Secret
Evil

Secret Evil

Zara Gill

EBURY
PRESS

Zara Gill is a pseudonym, and the identities of all people in the book have been disguised

1 3 5 7 9 10 8 6 4 2

First published in 2012 by Ebury Press, an imprint of Ebury Publishing
A Random House Group company

Copyright © Zara Gill and Jane Smith 2012

The Random House Group Limited Reg. No. 954009

Addresses for companies within the Random House Group can be
found at www.randomhouse.co.uk

A CIP catalogue record for this book is available from the British Library

Penguin Random House is committed to a sustainable future for
our business, our readers and our planet. This book is made from
Forest Stewardship Council® certified paper.

Printed and bound in Great Britain by Clays Ltd, St Ives plc

ISBN 9780091946760

To buy books by your favourite authors and register for offers visit
www.randomhouse.co.uk

This book is dedicated to my child, through whom I have learned the true meaning of unconditional love: I do love you, more than I can ever put into words; to my husband, for his support and understanding; to my mother-in-law, who has made me feel that I am part of a family; and to my mother: I love you, Mum.

Prologue

'GO HOME, PAKIS!' someone shouted from behind us. He sounded angry and, as I tightened my grip on the handle of the buggy, I glanced anxiously at Mum, who quickened her pace without raising her bowed head, so that I had to jog to keep up with her.

'We don't want darkies here.' It was another voice this time. I didn't really understand what he was saying, but there was no mistaking the sound of his hatred.

We were approaching the corner of what had become, just a few days earlier, 'our street', on a rough, run-down estate in a suburb of Manchester, when something whistled past my head, so close that the air it displaced felt like wind on my cheek. Then a stone about the size of my clenched fist skittered across the pavement in front of us.

Sami made a small whimpering noise, which echoed the one inside my own head, and I felt him pulling on the other handle of the buggy. Mum didn't look up or appear to change her pace, but by the time we reached the broken gate that hung from half a hinge at the end of the cracked-concrete path leading up to our front door, we were almost running.

Mum already had the key in her hand and, as soon as she'd turned it in the lock, she pushed Sami and me ahead of her into the house, heaved the buggy up over the step and slammed the door shut behind us. We stood in the hallway, listening for the sound of footsteps approaching the house and hearing only our own rapid breathing, and then Asha began to wail, twisting and turning in the buggy and raising her arms in an unspoken demand to be released.

For a moment, Mum continued to lean against the wall beside the door to the living room with her eyes shut, as though she couldn't hear Asha's cries. Then she sighed, shook her head dismissively and snapped, 'Will one of you get her out of the buggy, or do I have to do *everything*?' As she turned towards the front door and shot home the bolts that secured it, I bent down and tried to hook my shaking fingers around the clasp of the strap that was holding Asha's small, impatient body in the buggy.

Lifting my little sister into my arms, I asked Mum, 'What *are* Pakis? Why don't people like us?' They were questions I'd asked her more than a dozen times since we'd come to live in Manchester, and more than a dozen times she'd ignored them, as she did now.

'Go! Get out of my way,' she said, clicking her tongue irritably and almost snatching Asha out of my hands. She turned away from me and as she walked into the kitchen, I heard her mutter contemptuously, 'Pakis! Pakis! These people are ignorant. Have they never seen an Indian before?'

In the few weeks since we'd arrived in Manchester, we'd already moved several times, each time from one dismal, dirty flat to another. In fact, the house we'd just moved into wasn't quite as bad as all the other places we'd stayed, despite its air of grimy neglect, sparse, utilitarian furniture, damp walls, dented doors and dirty, stained carpets that you were reluctant to touch with your bare feet. What was even worse than the physical state of the house, however, was the sour smell that pervaded every room, filling your nostrils when you breathed in and clinging to the back of your throat so that you could taste it even when you were outside.

The hardest thing of all about being in Manchester wasn't the horrible places we'd lived in; or all the different schools my older brother Sami and I had been to, where no one wanted to be our friends; or the name-calling and stone-throwing that made my heart race with fear every time we set foot outside the house. What was worse than all those things was the fact that Dad wasn't with us, and I really missed him.

I rubbed the back of my hand across my cheeks to wipe away the tears of self-pity that were trickling down them and began to walk slowly up the stairs. I was halfway up when I heard Mum's voice drifting up from the kitchen and stopped to listen. It sounded high-pitched and querulous and I couldn't make out what she was saying, but then she laughed and, as I released the breath I hadn't realised I'd been holding, it felt as if the knot that seemed to have been tied around my stomach loosened just a little bit.

I ran up the last few stairs and along the landing to my mother's bedroom, where I wanted to look in the mirror that hung on the wall opposite her bed. My mother often told me that I was ugly. She'd sigh, as though I'd deliberately contrived to be 'ugly' in order to disappoint her, and say, 'Your skin is too dark and your eyes are almost black. How will I ever find a good husband for you?' Then she'd hold her hands out in front of her, palms upwards, in a familiar gesture of exasperation and I'd feel sick, the way I always did when I thought I'd made her unhappy.

At home in London, where we'd lived with Dad for the first seven years of my life – until just a few weeks ago – everyone agreed that my mother was beautiful. 'It's because I have pale skin and hazel eyes,' she'd tell me. And when I looked at her, I realised that my skin really *was* quite dark by comparison – certainly too dark for me to be considered beautiful by most Indians.

Despite what my mother said, I hadn't ever been consciously aware of other people's colour or race when we lived in London. At the school Sami and I had gone to there, almost *all* the children had skin of varying shades of brown or black, whereas at the schools we'd been to in Manchester – a different one each time we moved to another flat – there were very few non-white pupils. In fact, Sami and I were usually the only ones, and I'd begun to realise that, to some people at least, the colour of your skin mattered for reasons I didn't understand but that clearly had nothing to do with finding a 'good husband'.

So I often examined my face in the mirror in my mother's bedroom and prayed to any god that might be able to hear me, '*Please*, couldn't you make my skin just a *bit* lighter?' Because if my prayer was answered, it might make Mum happy, I might be able to make friends again, as I'd done so easily in London, and total strangers might stop shouting abuse and throwing things at me in the streets.

When I turned the handle on my mother's bedroom door, still thinking about our walk home from school, the memory of my fear was quickly replaced by surprise when the door failed to open. I stood rubbing the place on my head that had banged against it. I knew the door couldn't be locked, because my mother was in the kitchen with Sami and Asha. So I turned the handle again, this time pushing the door as hard as I could with my shoulder. When it flew open, I nearly tumbled headlong into the man who was standing in front of me, naked except for a towel that was wrapped around his waist.

Smiling, he held a stubby finger to his lips and whispered, 'Shhh.' Then he reached out his hand and pulled me into the room. I was still more surprised than afraid, but I instinctively twisted my shoulders and tried to slip out of his grasp, and for a moment the expression in his eyes seemed to change to one of cold anger.

Then he smiled again and said, in a voice that sounded amused, 'Don't look at me like that. Don't you remember me?'

Still holding my arm, he pulled me into the room, kicked the bedroom door closed and turned the key in the lock.

'I don't know you,' I told him, although there did seem to be *something* familiar about him.

'It's me!' he laughed. 'Surely you remember *me?*'

'You're Hassan,' I said at last. 'The lodger. What are you doing here? You live in London.'

'I *did* live in London.' He sounded almost like a child sounds when he has a secret he can't wait to tell you. 'And now I live here, in Manchester. In fact, as from today, I live *right* here, in this house, with you.'

What he was saying didn't make sense. How could he live with us? The house we'd recently moved into was larger than the squalid flats we'd lived in during the last few weeks – perhaps even larger than all of them put together – but there was no spare bedroom, and therefore nowhere for a lodger to stay.

'Mum won't let you,' I told him, with all the confidence of a seven-year-old. 'And she won't like it when she finds out you're here, in her bedroom. She didn't like it when you stayed with us in London. She was always asking Dad to tell you to leave and ...' I stopped, suddenly aware that what I was saying might be hurtful, or might even make him angry. But, to my surprise, instead of being offended, Hassan threw back his head and laughed again.

'Oh, she'll like it all right,' he said. 'In fact, *I'm* the reason she came here in the first place.'

Then, without any other warning that his mood had changed, he tightened his muscular fingers around my arm, leaned down until his face was on a level with mine and I could smell the stench of cigarettes on his breath, and hissed, 'It's a secret. Your mum will explain it to you tonight. Until then, you mustn't tell *anyone* that you've seen me. You have to promise.'

I don't know who he thought I *would* tell, because we didn't know anyone in Manchester. But he was clearly waiting for an answer. So I shrugged to show that I didn't care and said, 'I promise,' and when he released his grip on my arm, I wondered why I felt so anxious about the idea of his living with us.

Whenever I closed my eyes and wished that we were back at home in London with Dad – as I did countless times every day – I could sense something building up inside me that felt like panic. Before we'd come to Manchester, everything had made sense – or, at least, if it didn't, I'd never needed to worry about it because I knew that Mum and Dad would take care of us. But now it seemed that I didn't understand *anything*, and what was even worse was that Mum didn't seem to understand anything either.

Hassan sat on the edge of Mum's bed and pulled me down beside him. Then he touched my hair with his fingers in a way that made me feel uncomfortable. When I moved my head to look away from him, he took hold of my hand and said, 'Do you know what this is? Have you seen one of these before?'

I turned back towards him and gave a cry of disgust.

'Touch it,' Hassan said, laughing as he stood up and dropped his towel on to the floor. 'Go on. It won't bite you.'

'I don't *want* to touch it,' I told him. 'It's horrible. Let go of me or I'll tell Mum.'

As I tried to pull my hand away, Hassan twisted my wrist painfully and forced my fingers nearer to the revolting, swollen, blue-veined object between his legs.

'I told you to touch it,' Hassan said, and this time there was no trace of laughter in his voice.

'I'll tell Mum,' I sobbed again, clenching my fingers so tightly he'd probably have had to break them to unfurl them.

But instead of prising open my fist, Hassan suddenly let go of my hand, slid his fingers into my hair so that he could tilt my head backwards, forcing me to look up at him, and hissed at me, 'If you say anything to your mother, I will kill you.'

I thought he was going to hit me, and I blinked as his saliva spattered across my face. Instead, however, he struggled for a moment to regain control of his anger before saying, in a voice that sounded almost casual, 'This is our secret.' Then he picked up the towel, re-tied it around his waist and added, 'I am here to stay, and if you know what's good for you, you'll do what I tell you to do. If you don't, I can make your life *very* unpleasant.'

I was shaking as I fumbled to unlock the bedroom door, and when I stepped out on to the landing, Hassan said coldly, 'Remember, it's our secret.' Then he closed the door and I heard the key turn in the lock again.

There were several times that evening when I almost said something to Mum, but I ended up keeping the promise I'd made to Hassan.

Later, when Sami, Asha, Mum and I were sitting in the kitchen eating our supper, he walked in through the open door, smiling broadly. Mum smiled too when she looked up and saw him standing there. Then she glanced anxiously towards Sami and me and said, in the cajoling sort of voice adults sometimes use when they're trying to coax children to do something they don't want to do, 'You remember Hassan, don't you? Guess what! Such good news: he's going to live with us here. Isn't that wonderful?'

I stared at my plate and said nothing, but I knew from the delight I could hear in Sami's voice that he recognised Hassan immediately. In London, Sami had always called him 'my good friend'. He was copying the way our father sometimes talked about people, and it made me feel sad, because he'd always been a shy, awkward little boy who found it almost impossible to form relationships with anyone. So, even at the age of seven, I could sense that it was very important to him to believe that Hassan really was his friend.

When I looked up from my plate, my mother was watching me with a quizzical expression on her face. Then she shrugged and turned towards Hassan, and I closed my eyes and said silently in my head the words I'd whispered to myself over and over again during the last few weeks, although never before with such miserable intensity: 'I *really* miss you, Daddy. I wish you were here.'

Chapter One

MY MOTHER WAS thirteen and her sister fifteen when they came to England in the mid-1970s. They travelled together from the small town in India where they'd lived their entire lives. In fact, it was barely a town at all and although my mother's parents were quite well off in comparison to most of their friends, neighbours and other members of their families, the vast majority of its inhabitants were very poor.

I think my mother had had a happy childhood there. She must have been very frightened when the day came for her to leave everyone and everything that was familiar to her and set out on a journey of 5,000 miles to an unknown world full of strangers.

When my mother and her sister were sent to England to marry my father and his brother, neither of them had a birth certificate. So despite the fact that Mum was still only a child, all it took to enable her to marry a man who was eleven years older than she was – a cousin whom she'd never previously met – was one, simple lie about the date of her birth.

My father had come to England with his parents and brothers when he was ten years old. And, just like many other people who came to England from India at that time, he did nothing to correct the belief of the friends and family left at home that the streets of London were paved with gold. It was common knowledge that with a British passport and some hard work, anyone who went to England could prosper beyond their wildest imaginings. So my mother's parents must have considered the matches that had been made for their daughters to be very fortunate indeed.

Within days of arriving in this country, my mother's childhood came to an abrupt end. As well as becoming a wife to my father at the age of just thirteen, she also became a virtual slave to her coldly unsympathetic mother-in-law. From dawn till dusk, Mum cooked, cleaned and did the washing for everyone in the household, rarely setting foot outside the front door and never being consulted or asked her opinion about anything. And when she *did* go out – always accompanied by her husband or mother-in-law – she must have been disappointed to find that instead of the streets being paved with gold, as she'd expected them to be, they were grey and often soaked with rain.

Even when she fell pregnant just a few months after she was married, nothing changed for my mother. As the clothes she'd brought with her from India grew so tight across her rapidly expanding belly that sometimes she could barely breathe, she continued to spend her days on her hands and knees, doing the housework and whatever else her mother-in-law told her to do, trying to ignore her discomfort and the loneliness that seemed to have settled inside her like a weight alongside her unborn child.

When the baby was born, my father held his son proudly in his arms and thanked the gods for such a blessing. When my mother gave birth to a second son two years later, the gods were less kind and he lived for only a few days. Two years after that, I was born, and then, when I was four, my little sister, whose birth my father greeted with the comment, 'I can't believe you've shat out another girl. Perhaps it's time for me to take a second wife.'

Despite his unkindness to my mother on that occasion, I don't think Dad was generally unpleasant to her. Like most Indian men, he wanted sons and he simply saw no reason to hide his true feelings about becoming the father of a second daughter.

I think his mother's nastiness towards her daughter-in-law *was* often intentional, however, and I doubt that my mother shed a single tear when, one day shortly after I was born, my grandmother suffered a sudden heart attack and died.

It was the custom then – as it still is in many Indian families – for sons to continue to live with their parents after they were married and for their wives to take over most of the chores previously done by their mothers-in-law. But not long after my grandmother's death, when my grandfather married her sister, my parents were told that they were free to move out of the house and find somewhere to live on their own.

Dad's job in a factory wasn't very well paid, but he was determined to become a man of substance and someone worthy of respect. So he bought a large house not far from where my grandfather and step-grandmother lived and let out the rooms on the top floor to foreign students so that he could pay the mortgage.

Growing up surrounded by cousins, aunts, uncles, my grandfather and step-grandmother made me feel safe – as my mother must have done during her own childhood in India. Without being consciously aware of it, I knew that I belonged and that there was a place in the world into which I fitted exactly.

In some respects, nothing really changed for Mum after my parents moved into their own house, except that at least she was cooking and cleaning in her own home, for the benefit of her own family, without someone constantly looking over her shoulder and criticising everything she did. Even with the rent paid by the students, however, money was tight for my parents, until my father had the idea of buying a sewing machine so that my mother could work from home making clothes for a large company.

The work meant that Mum had even less time than she'd had before to spend with her children. But as she'd never paid us much attention anyway, I was happy playing with my brother and sister while Mum sat for hours at her sewing machine, stitching seams, securing buttons and glancing occasionally with satisfaction at the steadily rising pile of completed garments on the table beside her.

Even before Mum began to do the sewing, she hadn't had the time – or the inclination – to listen when I wanted to talk to her. After I started school, I brought home pictures I'd drawn and spelling tests for which I'd got full marks and tried to show them to her, and she'd always brush them aside without looking at them. One day, when I was very young, I ran out into the playground after school and told Mum proudly, 'My teacher says I'm good at spelling.' And I can still remember how deflated I felt when she snapped at me, 'Spelling? What's the use of being good at spelling? A man doesn't want a wife who knows how to *spell*. You're a girl; girls get married. That's what matters. Not spelling!'

Dad was almost equally indifferent to the things that mattered to us, except that although he didn't actually talk to us, he did let me chatter on excitedly when there was something I wanted to tell him, and the fact that he sometimes said, 'Yeah, yeah, okay – we'll sort that out,' at least made it *seem* as though he was listening to me.

Luckily, the lack of attention I received at home was more than made up for when I started school. I loved school. I looked forward to every single day I spent there and I'm sure that the encouragement my teachers gave me between the ages of five and seven made a huge difference to my self-confidence.

Indirectly, school had a good effect on Mum, too. Since coming to England, she'd learned almost no English – initially because she hadn't needed to: she'd never been allowed to go out of the house alone. But after my parents moved into their own house and my brother started going to the school across the road, he began to teach Mum the English words he learned, and gradually she became less isolated.

I loved my parents. Their love for me, however, was something I usually had to take on trust, because apart from Dad sometimes letting me sit on his knee, they never showed us any physical affection. I used to watch with envy as other parents greeted their children with hugs and kisses when they came out of school. But, to this day, Mum has never once put her arms around me and hugged me, let alone kissed me.

Dad only ever really spent any time with us on the relatively rare occasions when he took us to the park, and he only did *that* reluctantly, when Mum shoo-ed us out of the house because she had 'things to do'. At the park, I'd swing upside down from the bar in the playground calling incessantly, 'Watch me, Daddy,' while Sami stood anxiously to one side, looking miserable and dejected.

When I was a child, I didn't think about whether or not my parents loved us; I suppose I just took it for granted, in the same way that I accepted their almost total lack of parental common sense.

As children, we were simply white noise to Mum – always there as a constant, potentially or actually irritating presence on the periphery of her daily life, without registering fully on her conscious mind.

Because Mum had been married and had my brother, Sami, when she was just a child herself, there were lots of ways in which she'd never really grown up and gained an adult perspective. From a very young age, I was often left to entertain and look after my little sister, Asha, and Mum seemed to be completely unaware of the fact that I was much too young to do many of the things I did with her, such as making cakes and biscuits for her. Luckily, the disasters that often occurred were almost always culinary rather than involving physical harm.

I remember one morning when I was almost five years old. Sami had just left the house to go to school, Mum was settling down at the sewing machine and I was sitting on the floor with Asha when there was a knock on the front door. Mum sighed and clicked her tongue as she pushed her chair away from the sewing-machine table and walked out of the room and into the hallway. When she opened the front door, I heard a man's voice say, 'I'm very sorry. I've just hit your son with my car. He ran across the road right in front of me and I didn't have time to brake. Fortunately, I wasn't going very fast, and he says he's all right. I'm really *very* sorry.'

I left Asha on the floor in the living room and went

into the hallway, where I could see Sami standing silently beside the man, his head bowed and his arms wrapped tightly around his school bag.

'What's the matter with you?' Mum asked Sami and, despite the paleness of his face when he looked up at her, there was no trace of sympathy or concern in her voice as she added, 'Are you all right?'

Sami nodded his head without speaking.

'Well, come inside then,' Mum snapped irritably. She reached out her hand and I saw Sami wince as she grabbed his shoulder and pulled him roughly into the house.

'Thank you. Don't worry about it,' she said almost curtly to the man, who was still standing on the doorstep. And then she closed the door.

I don't think it even crossed Mum's mind to take Sami to hospital for a check-up in case he'd suffered any internal injuries. She simply didn't have the innate common sense or the learned knowledge to know that he might be seriously hurt in some way that wasn't visible or obvious. The fact that her son had been hit by a car was merely an inconvenience and an irritation that had taken her away from the pile of sewing that was waiting for her in the living room.

On another day, not long after I'd started going to

the school across the road with Sami, I woke up with a really bad stomach ache and diarrhoea. I felt terrible, but Mum – who never had any sympathy for other people's illnesses and ailments – told me not to make such a fuss and then almost pushed me out of the front door to go to school as usual.

By the time I'd walked the few hundred metres from our house to my classroom, my pants were soiled and I was almost rigid with embarrassment.

'I … I fell in dog poo on the way here,' I told my teacher when she wrinkled her nose and asked where the appalling smell was coming from. She must have realised immediately that that wasn't true, and she squeezed my hand and smiled at me as we waited together to cross the road that separated the school from our house.

'I'm afraid Zara's not at all well,' she said as soon as Mum opened the front door. But my stomach ache was nothing compared to the humiliation that washed over me like a wave of heat when Mum nodded her head and asked, without any echo of the sympathy I could hear in my teacher's voice, 'Oh, so do you think I should keep her in then?'

Dad's attitude to our health and well-being was even more vague and ill-informed than Mum's was, and he didn't have youthful ignorance as an excuse. It was probably just as well that he didn't play a very active role in our lives because he'd often do bizarre things without thinking. For example, one day when I was very little, he lifted me up off the ground and put me down on a radiator, only realising what he'd done when I started to cry because my feet were burning.

On another occasion, we all went out together to a local DIY shop and on the way home, Dad put Asha and me in the boot of his estate car without closing the door properly. We hadn't gone far when the boot door suddenly flew open and Asha and I tumbled out on to the road. For a moment, while my mind was trying to process what had happened, I just sat there, with my arms crossed, until the sound of Asha's screams and the pain in my bottom brought me back to my senses.

Thankfully, the car behind us swerved and somehow managed to miss us, and it was only the screech of its brakes that alerted Dad to the fact that the back of *his* car was wide open and both his daughters were sitting in the road, grazed and bruised.

It was the sort of thing he was always doing, and Mum often grumbled and complained about it bitterly. But she never seemed to do anything to try to counter-act his absentmindedness and make sure that we were all right.

Sami and I played together a lot and were very close when we were children. It was already clear that we were polar opposites in terms of our characters by the time I'd started school. Sami was quiet, with a fragile, nervous timidity that contrasted sharply with my own robust cheerfulness, and it was obvious that Dad favoured me. Dad sometimes referred to me as 'the son I never had'. What he approved of most, I think, were my endless supply of energy and my physical strength which, despite the four years' difference in our ages, was significantly superior to that of my brother.

Sami couldn't help being quiet and shy or not liking football, and the fact that he was timid and anxious and found it difficult to make friends meant that he needed the affection and approbation of his own family even more than most children do. But it was clear to everyone – including Sami himself – that Dad was disappointed with his only son, and instead of praising and encouraging him, he'd sometimes say, 'You're four years older than your sister, and you're a boy. Doesn't it make you ashamed that she's stronger and more capable than you are?'

It was a horrible, cruel thing to say, and I know that the way Dad treated Sami had a profoundly detrimental effect on his confidence and self-esteem. I sympathised with my brother and wanted to protect him, but I couldn't help relishing what I perceived to be my place at the centre of my father's affections.

I loved my father and I believed that, despite everything, he really cared about us. He did smack us occasionally when we were naughty, although his reprimands paled into insignificance in comparison to being chased round the garden by Mum waving a broom or a stick – or whatever else happened to come to hand. But neither of my parents ever really hurt us, and while I don't have many memories of my early childhood, I *do* remember that I was happy and that I felt secure.

In fact, the only really negative thing I remember about my childhood before the age of seven was the frustration and disappointment I used to feel at my parents' persistent, inexplicable refusal to celebrate our birthdays in any way. Every year, I'd tell them, 'All the kids at school get presents on their birthdays. So why can't I even have a cake?' Mum would just click her tongue and say, 'Go away! Go! Why are you always under my feet?'

Perhaps initially they didn't have enough money to buy us presents. But lack of money can't really have been the reason, because with what Dad was earning from his job at the factory, the income from Mum's sewing and the rent paid by the lodgers who lived on the top floor of our house, things did eventually get easier for my parents.

I must have been about six years old when Dad started talking about buying another property to let out. I know it was at about the same time as the Moroccan lodger, Hassan, moved in to live with us. He rented a room on the ground floor of our house, which my parents made into another bedroom, and from the start Mum didn't like him.

I don't know whether Dad would have taken any notice of Mum's complaints if he hadn't discovered that the new lodger was good at DIY. But once he knew that Hassan was able to turn his hand to almost any job from painting walls to fixing electrics, he told Mum excitedly, 'This lodger could not have moved in at a better time. His skills will be the key to my future good fortune.'

As an illegal immigrant, Hassan couldn't get legitimate paid work. So it was decided that in exchange for having all his meals provided for him and for paying only half the originally agreed rent, he would do work for my father around the house. Mum was furious. 'Get rid of him. I don't like him and we don't need him,' she told Dad.

Dad just shrugged, made an irritated whistling sound through his teeth and said, 'With his help, I will be able to buy another house. So give him whatever he wants to make him happy.'

'I don't like him,' Mum said again. 'And I don't want him living here. Get rid of him. Get him out of this house.'

'What are you talking about?' My father erupted suddenly into one of his rare outbursts of anger. 'Get rid of him? Why? He's exactly what I need to help me move forward with my plans. He pays rent *and* does work in the house. It's a perfect arrangement. So why would you even suggest getting rid of him? Be nice to him. It's business.'

Mum refused to explain her reasons and she continued to beg Dad at every opportunity, 'Get rid of this lodger. We don't need him and I don't like him.'

And I didn't like him either. Even at the age of six, I could sense that there was something about him that wasn't what it appeared to be. It often seemed as if he was two different people – sometimes patting Sami, Asha and me on the head and giving us sweets and at other times speaking sharply to us, or even smacking one of us when there was no one else there to see.

I remember one occasion when he smacked me and I

told him indignantly, 'You can't do that. You're not my dad, so you're not allowed to hit me.'

'I'm *allowed* to do exactly what I want,' Hassan said nastily, raising his hand as if to hit me again, just as Mum walked into the room behind him.

He didn't turn around or give any sign at all that he knew she was there. He simply slowed the movement of his hand and, instead of hitting me, patted me on the head. As he did so, he said, in a voice that was completely different from the one he'd just been using, 'That's right, Zara. Well done. You're a clever little girl, aren't you?'

I was still staring at him in open-mouthed bemusement when my mother told me to 'Run along and stop being a nuisance'. As I ran up the stairs to my bedroom, I felt that I'd been tricked in a way I didn't understand.

Although *I* didn't like him, Sami *did* and it seemed as if the lodger wanted to encourage Sami's belief that he was his friend, because he'd often buy him sweets and one day even came home with a second-hand bike for him.

We didn't have much contact with the lodgers who lived on the top floor of our house, except when they occasionally ate their evening meals with us. But because Hassan lived on the ground floor and Dad wanted to 'keep him sweet', he seemed to become more involved in our lives. He was always really nice when my parents were there, and sometimes did strange things when they weren't.

I became increasingly wary of him. Even if he didn't ever do anything really bad, he occasionally did things when no one else was around that you wouldn't expect an adult to do. For example, if I did something that annoyed him for some reason, he'd slap me or squeeze the skin on my arm tightly between his thumb and forefinger until I cried out in pain. I'd be so startled that I'd just look at him in shocked surprise, and he'd narrow his eyes, look back at me with an expression that was almost childishly triumphant, and apologise loudly for having hurt me 'accidentally'.

One day, when my cousins had come to visit us and we were playing in the garden, I went into the house to get a glass of water and Hassan came into the kitchen and hissed at me, 'I want them to go home. I don't want them here. So you'd better think of a way to make them leave.'

He was digging his fingernails into my skin and I felt suddenly frightened of him. As I tried to pull my arm out of his grasp, I told him, 'I *can't* make them leave.

Anyway, I don't want them to. I don't understand what you mean.'

'I just want them out of my house,' he said, and there was something in the expression on his face that stopped me telling him that it wasn't *his* house. Then my dad came into the kitchen and, as I escaped back into the garden, I could hear the lodger talking and laughing with him as if nothing had happened.

I think he actually wanted Sami and me to believe that he was mysterious. He always kept the door of his room firmly shut and told us never to open it, which was probably at least part of the reason why I became convinced that there was something in there he didn't want us to see and why, one day, I decided to find out what it was.

After Hassan had lived with us for a few months, it seemed that Mum finally accepted Dad's insistence that she should be nice to him. On this particular morning he was in the back garden with her, helping her to hang washing on the line; even so, my heart was racing as I tiptoed along the hallway towards his room and, very quietly, opened the door.

The smell of stale cigarettes and smoke was almost tangible and, for a moment, I stood in the doorway, pinching my nostrils tightly between my thumb and forefinger, trying not to gag. At the age of seven, my life was pretty much devoid of adventures of any kind, so just being somewhere I knew I shouldn't be was exhilarating. As my eyes began to adapt to the dim light that was filtering through the closed curtains at the window, I looked around the bedroom with a sense of excited trepidation.

Stepping carefully so that I didn't tread on the clothes and other discarded items that littered the floor, I tiptoed across the room and picked up a bottle from the wooden table under the window. It was full of a yellowy-grey liquid I couldn't identify, until I lifted the corner of one of the curtains to let more daylight into the room and realised that it was a mixture of water, cigarette butts and a thick layer of ash, which formed the sort of disgusting slurry you might find at the bottom of a dank, stagnant pond.

I replaced the bottle on the table and picked up one of several black-and-white photographs that were propped up against the lamp beside an overflowing ashtray on a small wooden chest, next to the unmade bed. Then, lifting the corner of the curtain again, I examined a picture of two elderly people with wrinkled, brown-skinned faces, who were standing next to what appeared to be a ruined stone building. The man looked like an older, less thickset version of the lodger, and I guessed that he and the woman in the picture were his parents.

I'd just put the photograph down and picked up another when I heard a sound behind me. I spun round and, as I did so, the photograph slipped out of my hand and floated to the floor.

'*What* are you doing?' the lodger demanded. 'How *dare* you come into my room? Get out! If you *ever* come in here again, I'll knock your block off.'

He didn't shout, or even raise his voice very much above its normal level, but the menace in his tone was clear, and I was instantly far more frightened than I'd have been if he *had* shouted at me.

'You … you can't hurt me,' I stammered, edging slowly sideways, away from the table, and trying to sound more confident than I felt. 'I'll tell my dad. You can't do anything to me. He won't let you.'

'You're a cheeky little bitch who needs to be taught a lesson,' Hassan retorted, making a grab for my arm as I dodged past him out into the hallway.

I don't think I saw my intrusion into his room and the fact that I'd been rooting around amongst his personal, private possessions as doing anything wrong, although I must have known that it wasn't actually 'right' for me to be there, particularly when he – and my parents – had told me so many times that it was strictly out of bounds. But I certainly hadn't expected him to be so angry, or for me to feel so scared.

Hassan's bedroom was at the front of the house, next to the front door, and if Mum was still outside in the back garden, I knew I wouldn't be able to reach her before he caught up with me. So, instead of heading for the back door, I sprinted down the hallway and into the living room, with the confused idea of being able to hide before he realised where I'd gone.

I'd only just flung myself down behind the sofa when he burst into the room. As I lay face down on the floor, squashed between the sofa and the cold metal of the radiator on the wall behind it, my heart was thumping.

'Little bitch,' Hassan hissed, kneeling on the sofa and leaning over the back of it as he tried to grab hold of me.

Pressing the palms of my hands down on to the floor, I tried to push myself up so that I could crawl out of the small space in which I was in danger of becoming trapped. Hassan swore and, as he reached down again, the movement of the sofa pushed my bent elbow between two of the vertical metal sections of the old radiator.

I screamed and tried to move my arm, but my elbow was stuck and struggling only made things worse.

'I'm *trying* to help you,' Hassan snapped at me, standing up and pulling the sofa away from the wall before tugging at my arm a couple of times until he managed to release it.

'You're *not* trying to help me,' I wailed. 'You shouldn't have chased me.'

The sharp pain that seemed to be radiating from my wrist to my elbow made me feel sick and, as I looked up into Hassan's face, I realised that his anger had been replaced by anxiety. I didn't for one moment think that his concern was for *my* well-being and, as if to confirm it, he said:

'It's your own fault. You shouldn't have gone behind the sofa and tried to get under the radiator. You got *yourself* stuck. *I* didn't do anything to hurt you. I was just trying to get you out.'

'You were only trying to get me out because you were angry and you were going to *do* something to me,' I sobbed. 'That's why I was frightened. And now my arm *really* hurts.'

I'd been trying not to cry but the pain was agonising, and when I burst into tears, he half carried, half dragged me out into the garden where he told my mother, in a voice full of false sympathy, 'She was behind the sofa. I didn't realise she was there, and when I sat down on it, she got wedged under the radiator and hurt her arm, poor thing. I don't know what she was doing there – playing a game with her brother, I suppose.'

Although my mother was always loud in her laments for her own misfortunes, she was never very interested in or sympathetic towards anyone else's, and her tone was impatient when she asked me what had happened. I glanced up at Hassan, who was looking at me with an expression of exaggerated concern that was belied by the cold threat in his eyes.

'I hurt my arm,' I sobbed in answer to my mother's question. 'It really, really hurts.'

And, for once, she took me, by bus, to the hospital, where my arm was X-rayed, found to be fractured and put in a cast, which I had to wear for the next few weeks.

I didn't really understand why Hassan had lied to my mother about what had happened. In one way, the whole thing *had* been an accident, because I don't think he'd intended to squash me against the wall when he knelt on the sofa. What had really frightened me at the time was the sense I'd had that when he found me in his room, his anger was almost out of control and that if he'd caught me when he chased me, he would have deliberately hurt me.

After a few months, it seemed that both my parents were changing their opinions about the lodger. My mother had stopped asking my father to make him leave, and sometimes even talked and laughed with him, but Dad seemed to be becoming increasingly irritated by him. Dad often complained about Hassan's apparent reluctance to do all the DIY jobs that needed to be done, as well as his tendency to interfere in matters that didn't concern him – such as telling Dad one day that he shouldn't speak to Mum in the way he had.

Despite Dad's misgivings, however, Hassan somehow managed to persuade him to buy another sewing machine so that he could work alongside Mum 'on the days when there aren't too many other jobs to do'.

'Are you crazy?' my auntie asked my father when she found out what he'd done. 'Are you going to leave your pretty young wife alone in the house all day with that man? Are you a simpleton, brother, that you can't see what's staring you in the face?'

Although my father *wasn't* a simpleton, he must have been very naïve, or perhaps just very trusting, because he shrugged his shoulders and said nothing until my auntie had gone, when he remarked mildly, 'That woman has venom in her tongue.'

It turned out that my father was wrong not to be

suspicious because, despite her earlier dislike of Hassan, my mother had fallen in love with him. She'd been plucked from her home and family in India when she was barely a teenager to marry a man she'd never met. She was unworldly and she'd never had a boyfriend before, or been in love. However, I think she'd have been happy for things to stay as they were, living with my father while continuing her affair. But Hassan had other ideas.

Perhaps the fact that he was cuckolding Dad gave Hassan the confidence to push for a more dominant position in our household. He miscalculated, though, when he mistook Dad's lack of suspicion about what was going on right under his nose for feeble-minded weakness. It wasn't long before my father showed himself to be understandably resistant to being pushed around in his own home, and he decided that the time had come for the lodger to move out.

Chapter Two

I CAN REMEMBER quite clearly the day Hassan left – or, at least, I can remember the huge rows my parents had. I'd never heard them arguing so angrily before. Almost as soon as they started to shout at each other, Sami and I scurried upstairs with Asha to the bedroom I shared with her. We sat on the beds, hardly breathing as we listened, even though some instinct told me that I didn't really want to hear what they were saying.

Mum was yelling at Dad about having sent the lodger away, and Dad was yelling at *her* because he thought that was what she'd wanted him to do.

'Didn't you keep insisting that you didn't like him and that you wanted me to get him out of the house?' he asked her furiously. 'Well, now I've done what you asked. So what possible reason could you have for being so angry with me? Despite the fact that I've already bought a second house and without the Moroccan I don't know how I'm going to get all the DIY work done so that I can let it out to tenants, I sent him away because *you* don't like him.' As he continued to shout, his voice became almost taunting as he said, 'Or is there some reason you want to tell me about that has made you change your mind?'

He paused for a moment as if waiting for Mum to answer, and then he bellowed, 'Well, is there? Is there some reason I should know about that made that man think he could talk to me as if I was nobody? Some reason he might have had for thinking that *he* could tell *me* what to do?'

Mum said something I couldn't hear and then they continued to shout and argue for what seemed like hours, so that my anxiety about how angry they were with each other far outweighed the relief I'd felt when the lodger left.

That night, Mum dragged a mattress into the downstairs room that used to be Hassan's and made Sami, Asha and me sleep there with her, while Dad slept alone in their bedroom upstairs.

For the next few weeks, we slept downstairs with Mum every night, and every day I became more and more miserable because I felt as if whatever I did I was upsetting one or the other of my parents. Mum and

Dad didn't speak to each other at all, except coldly when they had to, or, occasionally, when they argued some more. Dad would sometimes tell me that he was lonely without his family to keep him company, but if Mum saw me talking to him, she'd be hurt and upset, and then I'd feel *really* bad for having caused her even more distress. I was seven years old, it was the first time I could remember ever having felt so unhappy, and I didn't know what to do.

Then, one morning, Mum woke me up and told me to get dressed quickly because we were going on holiday. I'd never been away from home before, except to spend the occasional night at my grandfather's house, and I didn't really know what 'going on holiday' entailed.

'It's a school day,' I told Mum, sleepily. 'Am I going to school first?'

'No, not today,' she said, and there was something in her voice that woke me up properly and made it feel as if someone had just tied a little knot in my stomach. Mum was immediately impatient. 'I've told you, we're going on holiday,' she said, and then she added, in a falsely bright tone, 'we're going to Manchester.'

As I pushed back the covers on my bed, I felt more apprehensive than excited, because something didn't seem right. For weeks, my parents had barely spoken to each other, except angrily, and now, overnight, everything had apparently changed and we were all going to go away on holiday together. I supposed it was possible: I knew that adults sometimes did some very strange things that it wasn't worth trying to understand.

I was still in my bedroom getting dressed when Mum bustled in again and handed me a Tesco carrier bag. 'It's for the things you want to take with you,' she told me. 'But hurry. We have to go. Be quick!' She sounded nervous, almost panicky, and I felt the little knot in my stomach tighten.

While Mum pulled underwear, socks and night-dresses out of my chest of drawers and stuffed them into another carrier bag, I grabbed my favourite red jumper and red chequered dress, and then snatched up from the table beside my bed the pencil case in the shape of a piano keyboard that my grandfather had bought for me.

'How long will we be away?' I asked Mum. 'What *is* Manchester? Has Dad gone to work? Is he coming with us?'

'Yes, he's gone to work,' my mother snapped, reaching out her hand to smack the side of my head. 'Now just get ready and stop making such a fuss. You'll like Manchester, and we'll come back here after a while.'

There was something about the way she said the last sentence that made me look at her quickly and ask, 'Dad isn't coming, is he? When will we see him again?'

Mum didn't answer.

A few minutes later, when I went downstairs, clutching my overstuffed carrier bag in both hands, she was standing in the kitchen, chewing at the end of a pencil and staring at a piece of paper that was on the table in front of her.

'Can I write a note to Dad?' I asked her. She sighed as she pushed the piece of paper and the pencil across the table towards me. Then she walked quickly out of the room.

'*Dear Dad,*' I wrote. '*I'm going to miss you. But I'll come back soon.*'

Was that true? I wondered. *What if I never saw my dad again?* Even as the thought entered my head I knew that it was ridiculous, because people don't just leave their dads and go away forever. Even so, I crossed out the words I'd written and started again.

'*Dear Dad, we are going away for a few days. I wish you were coming with us.*'

That didn't sound right either. So, again, I scribbled it out, and I was still trying to decide what to write when Mum came back into the kitchen.

'*Why* are we going without Dad?' I asked her. 'When will we come home again? I don't know what to write to him.'

'I don't *know* when we'll come home,' Mum said, and for a moment I thought she'd been crying. Then she sounded impatient again as she added, 'Come on. We've got to go – *now*. Get your things.'

Although I was infected by the urgency I could hear in her voice, I couldn't bear the thought of leaving without writing *something* to Dad, because I knew he'd be really sad that he hadn't been able to go with us. So I scrawled hastily, '*I'm going to really miss you, Dad. I love you and I promise I'll come home again soon.*'

Mum waved her hands at me, as if to shoo me out of the kitchen, and then she pushed me ahead of her into the hallway, where Asha was already strapped into the buggy, its handles festooned with bulging carrier bags. Sami was standing nervously clutching a carrier bag to his chest, the pupils of his eyes magnified by unshed tears.

As we walked out of the front door and hurried along the pavement away from our house, I could hear the sound of children playing in the playground of my school across the road. *I wish I was there with them,* I thought. *I'd rather be in the playground with my friends than going on a holiday.* I could feel tears pricking my eyes too, because even though Mum had said that we were going on an adventure, she was so clearly upset and anxious that it didn't *feel* like a good thing.

Wishing that Dad was with us was a feeling that grew stronger when we arrived at the tube station, because it soon became clear that Mum didn't know what to do. It was the first time she'd ever been anywhere with us on her own, except to do the shopping or visit aunts and uncles, and she still didn't speak very good English. So Sami had to buy the tickets, with the money she pushed into his hand, and then find the way to the platform where we would be able to catch a train to Euston.

I don't think I'd ever sensed uncertainty in my mother before that day. But I could see that she was as frightened as I was as we listened to the sound, that began as a distant rattling, grow to become a roar and then watched as a train burst out of the tunnel at the end of the platform.

No one stopped to help Mum and Sami as they struggled to lift the overladen buggy into a carriage, or when we almost fell out of the train as the doors opened at Euston. Before we had a chance to catch our breath, we were being dragged along in the wake of all the impatient people who were hurrying along the platform and I was clinging to the buggy as if my life depended on it. Someone did help Mum lift the buggy on to the escalator, and I stood on the step behind her, clutching the wide black handrail with both hands and praying that I wouldn't topple backwards and fall.

Somehow, we found our way to the mainline station and ended up on the right platform. As the train sped through the outskirts of London and into open country-side, Sami and I pressed our noses against the window to watch the passing of a world we'd never even known existed, and I finally began to feel excited.

I tried to imagine what Manchester would be like. I hadn't ever been more than a few miles away from our house in London, so I didn't really understand that there were other towns in other parts of the country. The picture that began to form in my mind was of a massive room, like a town hall I'd been into once with Dad. It had a shiny wooden floor, which reflected the sunlight flooding in through vaulted windows that reached almost to the ceiling. In 'Manchester', however, unlike the town hall, there was a row of beds along each of the two longest walls, where all the mothers and children who were on holiday slept at night under thick, fluffy duvets, their heads resting peacefully on fat, white, feather pillows.

And that was when it suddenly struck me that *that* was why Dad wasn't coming with us: Manchester must be a place where only mothers and their children could go, because there was nothing there for dads to do and they'd be bored. It was an explanation that made perfect sense to me, and as soon as I'd thought of it, I felt better, although I still would have preferred to be going somewhere that dads could go too.

We were on the train for more than three hours. When we finally tumbled off it into cold, almost horizontal rain that stung our faces, Asha began to wail and I suddenly felt angry with my mother. It was obvious that she'd made a mistake and we'd got off the train at the wrong station – and it was obvious, too, that she wasn't really in control of what was happening to us; the thought made me feel sick.

'Why did we get off the train here?' I asked her crossly, trying to wipe the rain off my face with a wet sleeve.

'Because *this* is Manchester,' Mum answered, and the weary despondency I could hear in her voice made my stomach churn with anxiety.

'No!' I almost shouted at her. '*This* isn't Manchester. This isn't the place where all the mothers take their children for a holiday.'

I could feel panic rising up inside me: Mum had made a terrible mistake and had brought us to the wrong place, which meant that I couldn't rely on her as I'd always done before, without thinking. But all she said was 'Hurry' and then she turned and followed the last few people with their bags and briefcases and click-clacking heels who were walking purposefully along the platform, apparently oblivious to the driving rain and bitterly cold wind that seemed to penetrate into every corner of the station.

I hadn't ever been in a taxi before, but I was too wet, miserable and anxious to be excited by what, in any other circumstances, would have been an adventure. As I stared out of the window without really seeing anything, I could sense that Sami was distressed, too.

Before we'd got into the taxi, Mum had handed the driver a soggy, crumpled bit of paper, which must have had an address written on it. A few minutes later, he stopped outside a grim house with a broken sign above its front door and said, 'This is it. Good luck.'

We stood on the pavement outside the dismal house while Mum handed the taxi driver some money through his open window. Then he smiled a small, rueful smile, said 'Good luck' again, and drove away.

After Mum rang the bell that was hanging by just one

rusty screw beside the front door of the house, we watched through a small, cracked pane of glass as a sour-faced woman shuffled through the dark hallway towards us. When the woman opened the door and Mum had lifted Asha out of the buggy, we followed her down a dimly lit corridor that smelled of damp and hot cooking oil, and I had to bite my lip to stop myself bursting into tears.

Without saying a word to us, the woman managed to convey the impression that we weren't the sort of guests she was used to having in her hotel – which seemed unlikely, even allowing for the fact that we looked like a sodden, raggle-taggle band of itinerants: it clearly wasn't the sort of place anyone would *choose* to stay, unless they were down on their luck and had run out of other options.

Even in the dull light from the single, unshaded light bulb that hung from a greasy, frayed cable above our heads, I could see clearly the stains on the threadbare carpet as the woman walked ahead of us up the stairs. She stopped on the first landing, opened a door and flicked a light switch on the wall, and we stood silently on the threshold of a small, dismal room that appeared to be crammed full of beds.

The bare light bulb in the room was even dimmer

than the one on the stairs, but not dim enough to hide the layer of dust that covered every flat surface, or the patches of effervescing damp on every wall. The most peculiar thing about the room, however, was the fact that everything in it – its walls and ceiling, the battered chest of drawers, tatty bedding and an incongruously shell-shaped washbasin in one corner – was pink.

We stood in silence, all of us apparently sharing the same reluctance to step inside the room, because doing so would mean that we'd accepted the fact that we were actually going to sleep in it. And we were still standing in the doorway when the woman waved her hand along the corridor and said, 'Bathroom's second door on the right. Hot water from seven to eight in the mornings, six to seven in the evenings.' Then she pushed a key into Mum's hand, turned her back on us and stomped down the stairs.

As soon as she'd gone, I burst into tears and threw myself, face down, on to the pink blankets on one of the beds.

'I want to go home,' I sobbed. 'And I want my *daddy*.' Mum just clicked her tongue and told me to go downstairs with Sami and help him bring up the buggy and carrier bags.

Later, after Mum had inspected the communal bathroom next to our room, she told us that we mustn't, under any circumstances, use the shower. So, for the next few days, we washed in the hideous pink basin in our bedroom. In fact, despite the miserable squalor of the hotel, we spent most of the next week in the bedroom, because we soon discovered that every time we went out, we were the focus of interest that was often overtly hostile.

I soon realised that I'd been wrong about Manchester. It wasn't the large, sun-drenched room of my imagination, where women and their children went on holiday. It was a city, a bit like London except that, in the late 1980s, there didn't seem to be many other Asian or black people living there, which was apparently why we attracted so much unfriendly attention and why some people actually stopped and stared at us whenever we walked down the street.

We couldn't cook our own food in the pink hotel and most of our meals consisted of sandwiches, which we bought in the local shop and ate in our room. And then, one day, Mum took us to eat at a café. We sat down at a table near the counter and then Mum pushed money into Sami's hand and told him to order fish and chips for all of us. Sami hated having to talk to strangers, but I don't think he minded so much on that occasion, because eating in a café was a huge and rare treat.

A few minutes later, when the woman brought plates piled high with steaming hot food to our table, I felt the first stirrings of anxiety, because I knew immediately that Sami had made a mistake and that Mum couldn't possibly afford to pay for what he'd ordered. To my amazement, however, instead of slapping Sami's head and telling him he was stupid, Mum waved her hand at me and said, 'Eat! Eat! Staring at your plate won't fill your stomach.'

In the few days since we'd arrived in Manchester, I'd already begun to feel a strange sense of detachment from my 'real' life in London. I hadn't known that there were so many things I didn't understand and, clearly, Mum buying us fish and chips in a café was just another one of them. In fact, it was the first *good* thing that had happened since we'd left home, and although it didn't make up for all the bad things, at least it meant it was possible that other good things might happen, too.

I was halfway through my plate of food when I suddenly became aware that someone was standing beside our table. I looked up and then glanced at Mum, who was smiling – for the first time since before we'd left London. The man was smiling too and, as he picked up a chair from the empty table next to ours, he said something I couldn't hear and Mum actually laughed. And that was when I realised it was Hassan, the lodger from London, who, for reasons I hadn't understood, had been the cause of the worst arguments Mum and Dad had ever had.

Most children accept most things that adults do without really wondering how or why they do them, and I don't think I gave much thought to how Hassan came to be sitting at our table in a café in Manchester, when we'd last seen him at our house in London. In any case, I was far more interested in eating my fish and chips than I was in Hassan. So I barely heard what he and Mum said to each other and, when he left the café a few minutes later, I instantly forgot all about him.

The next morning, when we woke up in the pink hotel, Mum told us to pack all our things into the carrier bags because we were leaving. An hour later, we drew up in a taxi outside a small, double-fronted Victorian house that was partially hidden from the street by a hedge that was growing through the broken slats of a wooden fence.

Like the other taxi driver had done when he left us outside the pink hotel on our first day in Manchester, the man smiled almost pityingly at us as he said, 'This is the place.' And once again my heart sank as we pushed open the gate and walked up the path to the front door.

Although I didn't really understand what it meant at the time, the house was a refuge for women and their children who'd escaped from violent men. Amongst them there was just one other non-white woman – a Pakistani woman with her two children – who quickly made it clear that she, like everyone else living there, didn't want anything to do with us.

I couldn't work out why everyone seemed to dislike us so much – even before they'd spoken to us – and why we were staying there at all. *Our* dad never hit us, or Mum, so there didn't seem to be any need for us to be in a 'safe place'.

Ironically perhaps, my aunt – the sister Mum had travelled with from India and who'd married my father's older brother – *was* beaten by her husband, so regularly and severely that she tried to kill herself on more than one occasion. In that respect at least, Mum was lucky by comparison.

For whatever reason, we stayed at the refuge and Sami and I went to a nearby school – where no one wanted to be my friend, however hard I tried to be like-able, and where none of the other kids spoke to us except to call us names. It was something else to add to the rapidly growing list of things I didn't understand.

At home in London, I'd always felt that I was the

same as all the other children at school – not that I'd ever really even thought about it. But in Manchester, everyone – the children at school, as well as many of the children and adults we encountered on the streets – made it clear that we were different and unwelcome. For the first time in my life, I felt like an outsider.

What was even worse was the feeling that there was absolutely nothing I could do about any of it. For as long as I could remember before we went to Manchester, everything in my life had just *happened*. I lived with Mum, Dad, Sami and then, from the time I was four, Asha. We visited other members of our family at their houses, or they came to ours. I went to school, where I had friends and where the teachers were nice to me and made me feel good about myself. Everything just sort of worked, without my even having to think about it.

In Manchester, however, everything was different. Mum was unhappy and didn't seem to know what to do about *anything*, and the more aware I became of how completely out of her depth she was, and that she was no more able to control anything than *I* was, the more anxious and frightened I felt.

We'd been living at the refuge for about four weeks when the council moved us into a small flat on a run-down estate of houses with broken or boarded-up windows and gardens full of overflowing rubbish bins. When we moved, Sami and I started going to another school, nearer our new home, and I allowed myself to believe, with all the optimism of childhood, that things were going to improve.

Chapter Three

THERE'D BEEN LOTS of black and Asian children at our school in London and I don't remember ever being consciously aware that I was different from *any* of them, or from the white kids either. But there were just two other non-white kids at our new school – both of them black – and by the time we moved into the flat being called names like 'Paki' and 'Bud Bud' (supposedly the sound Indians make when they talk) had become part of my new life.

On the morning when we'd left our home in London, I'd listened to the sound of all the children playing in the playground at my school across the road and wished I could be there with them. Now the school playground had become somewhere I dreaded being. Every break time, I'd stand against the wall of the school building and try to flatten myself into invisibility, while the other children pointed and shouted at me, 'Hey, Paki, did your mum make your clothes? They look like she did. I bet she can't afford to *buy* you proper clothes.'

Although I had to concentrate *really* hard to stop myself bursting into tears, I did have to admit that they had a point, because Mum made me wear clothes that couldn't have been better designed if their purpose had actually been to make me stand out and look odd. At home in London, apart from celebrating the main Muslim religious festivals with all our aunts and uncles, Mum hadn't ever shown any real interest in other aspects of the Muslim religion, or observed its customs. But in Manchester, she insisted that whenever I went out of the house, my legs had to be covered.

I had to wear a uniform for school, so Mum went to a charity shop and bought me a cheap green skirt that was several sizes too big for me, and then made me a pair of baggy leggings – out of a piece of shiny, ugly, white material she'd bought at the local market – which she insisted on my wearing under the skirt. I might just as well have hung a sign around my neck saying 'Tease me. I'm different'. And different was the one thing more than any other that I didn't want to be. There was no denying that the outfit looked ridiculous

– primarily because of the marked contrast between the whiteness of the trousers and the sludgy green colour of the skirt.

As if that wasn't humiliating enough, Mum also insisted on putting oil in my hair, which is a custom among Asian women but which to the other children at school – almost none of whom had ever seen an Indian girl before – just made my hair look greasy and unwashed.

At first, I don't think I really believed that the other children didn't like me simply because of the colour of my skin. So, despite all the handicaps Mum thought up for me, I didn't give up hope that if I tried hard enough, someone would eventually like me. I was constantly trying to think of ways to make that happen – always without success.

At least at school they only called me names and refused to sit next to me, whereas in the street people sometimes threw stones and eggs at us. Their hostility towards us was as frightening as it was baffling to me, and I simply didn't understand *why* they were so angry and full of hatred.

We only stayed in that first flat on the estate for a couple of weeks because the other tenants in the building complained that we were noisy, and the council moved us on. I expect we did sometimes make quite a lot of noise – three children shut inside a tiny flat for hours on end. Or maybe what the neighbours *really* didn't like was having a family of 'darkies' living in the same house with them, and they had the sense to realise that 'excessive noise' would be a more acceptable complaint to make to the council.

When we were moved out of that flat and into another one, on an almost identical council estate, we moved schools too. But the next school was just the same, and so was the next one and the one after that.

There was one council estate, where we lived for a while during the first couple of months, which made all the racism we'd previously encountered seem half-hearted. It was what they called a 'sink estate', and almost everyone who lived there seemed to have serious problems. There were dogs as well as aggressive teenagers roaming the streets and, after I was hit on the head by a football someone kicked at me when we were walking back from the shops with Mum one day, we became afraid to set foot outside our own front door.

Something that would have made us stand out as different in London but that was almost the norm on that particular estate was the fact that we were 'fatherless'. There seemed to be almost no adult males living there at all, which someone told Mum was because most of them were in jail and serious crime was a way of life there. I don't think Mum really believed her until our elderly neighbour was murdered when someone broke into his house.

When we left that estate, we moved to yet another run-down, dismally depressing area of town where Sami and I had to start at another school. Once again, we were the only Asians.

Every morning, when I woke up, I'd lie in bed for a few seconds, waiting for my brain to push its way up through whatever dream I'd been having, and then my heart would start to thud and, after a few more seconds, I'd remember why: I dreaded going to school.

It wasn't just the colour of my skin that set me apart and made other children refuse to sit next to me in class: it was the smell. I could smell it too, and I was mortified – as well as mystified – by it. Every day, when I walked into the classroom, the other children would pretend they hadn't seen me and they'd start to sniff. Then they'd hold their noses and one of them would say, dramatically, 'What *is* that disgusting smell?' And while everyone else laughed, they'd turn around, pretend to notice me for the first time, and ask, 'Is that horrible smell coming from you? It is! You really *stink*.'

Every single day I'd feel my face go hot with embarrassment and shame and I'd have to swallow hard a few times to try to stop myself crying before I said, 'No. *No*, it isn't me.' Then I'd make an excuse – the same one I'd made on the day Mum sent me to my school in London when I had diarrhoea: 'It's just dog poo; I trod in it on the way to school and I can't get the smell off my shoes.' Everyone would laugh again, hold their noses and turn their backs on me. And I knew I couldn't blame them, because they were right: I *did* smell. But I didn't know what to do about it.

Looking back on it now, I can't believe that Mum let me go to school like that. She couldn't do anything about the colour of my skin and she couldn't stop people shouting abuse at us – although not making me wear white trousers under a green skirt might have helped a bit – but she *could* have done something about the smell.

When we lived in London with Dad, Mum did all the cooking and the housework; in Manchester, however, things were different. She still fed us regularly – and as well as she could afford to do on the small amount of benefit money she was getting – but she didn't clean the house and, more importantly for me, she stopped gathering up the dirty clothes and washing them. She didn't show us how to do it ourselves either, so when I woke up every morning and found the clothes I'd worn the day before still lying on the chair beside my bed where I'd left them, I put them on again.

I can't believe now that it didn't even cross my mind to wash my clothes myself – although I *was* only seven – and it wasn't long before I reeked.

I asked my mother quite recently why she'd allowed that to happen, and she told me, 'When I was seven years old, I had two school uniforms. I wore one of them one day and the other the next, and every night I washed the one I'd just worn by hand and hung it out to dry. So that's what I expected you to do.' She didn't seem to understand what I meant when I told her that that would have been fine, if only she'd explained it to me at the time.

I can see now that Mum was probably depressed, so maybe she wasn't aware of what was happening to Sami and me every day and how miserable we were. I don't think that was the only explanation, however; she just wasn't a very competent parent, and in some ways – perhaps in the ways that matter most to a child – we *were* quite neglected, and that had a bad effect on all of us.

Sami's shy nervousness was exacerbated when we moved to Manchester, and he became even more anxious and introverted. I think that my own change in character must have been very obvious too, because, whereas I'd always been confident and full of cheerful energy, it wasn't long before I'd become fearful and withdrawn – a timid observer rather than the enthusiastic participant I always used to be.

I did make one friend in one of the places we lived for a while. She was a Pakistani girl who lived nearby and she used to play with me and tell me about her family – which sounded as though it was very different from mine. I always made huge efforts to be likeable, because I was so desperate for *someone* to like me, and having even one friend made almost everything seem better.

Then we moved again, and I wrote a letter to my friend to tell her that I couldn't give her my new address because my mum didn't want my dad to find out where we were. I didn't understand how or why my friend would tell my dad – who she didn't know – where we were living, but Mum was adamant. '*I really miss not having a friend any more,*' I wrote in my letter, which didn't even begin to convey how distressed I really felt.

*

When Mum left Dad, our lives changed, quite literally, overnight. One night I'd gone to bed in our house in London, and the next night I'd slept in the horrible pink hotel in Manchester. And even though I felt very miserable at the time, I'm sure I would have felt far worse if I'd had any idea just how dramatically and irrevocably the life I'd always known would change just a few weeks later.

Mum didn't want Dad to know that we were in Manchester, so we weren't allowed to phone him in case we said something that might give him a clue about where we were. I missed him *really* badly. Every time Sami or I asked Mum when we were going to see him again, she just said, 'Soon,' but she never looked at us when she said it, and I began to wonder if she was telling us the truth.

Eventually she *did* set up a meeting with Dad, and I could hardly contain my excitement at the thought of seeing him again. The place where we were going to meet him was so far away from where we were living that we had to travel there on two different trains and three buses. Throughout the journey I sat in silence, trying to remember the whole list of things Mum had told us we mustn't say to him, and by the time we arrived, my head was spinning and I was almost afraid to open my mouth at all.

If Mum had told me to keep a secret from Dad before we'd gone to live in Manchester, I'd have been surprised and I wouldn't have thought twice about asking her why. Fewer things surprised me by that time, however, and I'd already learned that it was best not to ask questions and just to do what I was told.

The room in the ugly concrete building where Dad was going to meet us looked a bit like a sparsely furnished doctor's waiting room. He wasn't there when we arrived, but when the door opened a few minutes later and he was standing there, looking almost nervous, I hurled myself almost horizontally across the room towards him. When he bent down, I wrapped my arms around his neck, buried my head in his shoulder and burst into tears.

When Mum first told us that we were going to see Dad, I'd stopped praying for that every night and had begun to pray instead that he'd take us back to London with him. I'd often imagined the scene in my head: he hugged Mum and then me, Sami and Asha, and told us how much he'd missed us and how happy he was to see us all again. In fact, I'd been so certain that he'd take us home with him that I'd put the pencil case that looked like a piano keyboard in the pocket of my coat, because it was the one possession I didn't want to leave behind. So I was heartbroken when it soon became clear that the only reason Dad had come at all was because he wanted to talk to Mum and that Mum didn't want to talk to him.

For the next hour, while Sami, Asha and I sat on the floor and played with the scuffed and broken toys we'd found in a box underneath a low, wooden table, Dad barely spoke to us – and barely seemed to hear us when *we* spoke to *him*. There was a voice in my head that kept saying, 'This wasn't how it was supposed to be. *Do* something. Make him notice you so that he'll remember you're like the son he never had.' But I couldn't think of anything to do and, as the realisation slowly dawned on me that Dad didn't really care about us any more, the tears spilled out on to my cheeks again.

What I'd imagined Dad saying to me wasn't too far removed from what he actually said to Mum, as he told her, 'Come home with me. I don't care what people say. It doesn't matter if they think you've brought shame and disgrace on the family. I miss you and I want you to come home.' But Mum didn't answer as I would have done. She shook his hand off her arm and said 'No', and eventually Dad stood up, said something to

Mum in a low voice, so that I couldn't hear, and left the room without a backward glance.

I sat there for a few minutes after the door had closed, watching and waiting for Dad to come back. Then we put on our coats and walked out on to the unfamiliar street.

Back in the dismal house in Manchester, I lay on my bed and sobbed. I was certain that nothing would ever happen again that would make me happy. I'd begun to be afraid that everything that ever happened in the future – however good I might think it was going to be – would turn out to be a bad thing after all.

Gradually, as the weeks passed and our lives began to settle into some sort of new normality, I think I stopped being actively unhappy, although missing Dad still felt like a physical pain. And then Hassan, our lodger from London – who my mother had hated and then liked, and who my father had liked and then been angry with and told to leave – moved in to live with us in our house in Manchester and everything changed, forever.

From the day he left our house in London until he opened the door of my mother's bedroom in the house in Manchester, I'd barely given Hassan a single thought. When he came into the café when we were staying at the pink hotel, I don't think I consciously absorbed the fact that it was him. And I had absolutely no idea that ever since we'd arrived in Manchester, while Sami and I were at school every day, Mum had been seeing him. It wasn't until years later that I realised his being in Manchester wasn't a coincidence at all, and that *he* was the reason Mum took us away from Dad. Which meant that it was because of him – or, at least, because Mum wanted to be with him – that we had no money and were living in horrible, filthy places in a world where everyone hated us and where I woke up every morning with my heart thudding and something squeezing my stomach so that I felt sick and didn't want to get out of bed.

'Did you miss me after I left your house in London?' Hassan asked me that first day, after he'd locked the door of the bedroom and told me I mustn't tell anyone he was there.

'No, I don't think so,' I said. 'But I think my brother did.'

And even then, before I really knew Hassan, some instinct told me that it would be better not to say aloud the thought that was in my mind: *I wish you hadn't come back into our lives again.* I might have forgotten about him for the last few months, but I soon remembered how frightened he sometimes used to make me feel.

At home in Morocco, Hassan had been a priest, a *mawlānā*, and whilst he was an illegal immigrant in this country and so couldn't get a legitimate job, he sometimes performed ceremonies for his Muslim friends, for which they paid him a small amount of money – but never more than enough to keep him in cigarettes for a few days. So, after he moved in to live with us, Mum had to support him, and as she was already struggling to feed and clothe herself and her three children on the money she received in state benefits, things quickly became even harder for us financially than they'd been before he came.

We saw Dad a few more times after the first meeting, until he finally accepted the fact that Mum wasn't going to go back to him and didn't come again. In time, I learned that although the ache of loss never really goes away, you can live with almost anything in the end.

There were some things I was never going to get used to, however, and when Mum told me one day that Hassan wanted us to call him 'Dad', I refused.

When Hassan first moved in with us in Manchester, he tried to make us like him in the same way he'd done in London, by joking with us and buying us sweets. He even came home one day with a computer and some games – which should have made him Sami's 'good friend' for life. But I *didn't* like him and even if I had, calling him Dad would have felt like shrugging my shoulders and accepting the fact that my real dad wasn't ever coming back into our lives.

'I won't do it,' I told Mum. 'He's not our dad and he shouldn't be here. Dad wouldn't like it if he knew.' I had no real grounds for saying what I said, but the look that flashed across Mum's face seemed to confirm that I was right.

Perhaps an even more important reason why I didn't want Hassan to be my new father was because it had quickly become apparent that he had a ferocious temper. Sometimes, even the smallest irritation could make him explode into physical violence. Looking back on it now, it seems ironic that he'd arranged for us to stay in a refuge for battered women and their children when we first arrived in Manchester, at a time when we were probably the only people there who *hadn't* been battered and abused. Now, that was about to change.

Hassan would fly into rages, often for no apparent reason. Sometimes he'd hurt us inadvertently, for example if we just happened to be standing in the way when his rage erupted and he picked up the nearest heavy object and hurled it across the room. But he'd also lash out at Sami or me – or, when she was a bit older, Asha – sometimes knocking us out of a chair and on to the floor. While we were still trying to work out what had happened, he'd start shouting at us about something we didn't know we'd done – and wouldn't have known was 'wrong' even if we had. Then he'd beat us repeatedly and viciously, while Mum flapped her hands and told him, feebly, to stop.

His anger was like a wild animal that, suddenly unleashed, destroyed everything in its path. He didn't *seem* to be able to control it, but he didn't hit Mum, so maybe it wasn't completely uncontainable, or maybe he really did love her.

It sometimes seemed to me that Mum didn't love *us*, because if she did I couldn't understand why she didn't realise that she should be doing whatever it took to protect us from Hassan's terrible, unpredictable temper and his vicious assaults. In fact, it was the unpredictability of Hassan's temper that was almost worse than anything else, because you were always watching and waiting for him to explode into anger about something, which meant that you could never relax.

I was seven years old, unhappy at home and at school, my stomach constantly churned and tied itself into painful knots of anxiety. If someone had asked me to do so, I wouldn't have been able to think of one single positive thing about my life.

And then, one day, out of the blue, Mum gave me a rabbit.

Chapter Four

I THINK SOMEONE had given the rabbit to Mum because they couldn't look after him, but at the time I didn't even stop to wonder *where* he came from. I simply couldn't believe it when I came home from school one day, walked into the kitchen and saw first the hutch and then long white whiskers and a little pink, twitching nose poking through the wire mesh.

Mum had followed me into the kitchen and was standing with her back to me at the sink when I ran across the room, opened the door of the hutch and picked up the rabbit. She still didn't say anything when I sat down on the floor, held him tightly against my chest so that I could bury my face in his soft, white fur, and imagined he was mine.

I'd always loved animals, but I'd long ago given up asking if we could have a pet. So when I asked Mum, 'Who does he belong to? Is he ours? Can we keep him?'

I thought I already knew the answers to my questions. Which is why I didn't immediately understand what she said when she turned, clicked her tongue impatiently and told me, 'You have to take care of him yourself. You have to feed him and change his bedding every day so that it doesn't smell. If you don't, I'll give him away to someone else.' Then it slowly dawned on me that the rabbit was mine and that all I had to do to be able to keep him was feed him and clean out his hutch. Mum made them sound like tiresome chores, but to me they'd be a pleasure, because having a pet of my own to take care of would mean that there'd be something for me to look forward to every day. And if I had something of my own to love, I knew that the bullying and teasing at school, and the taunts and abuse that were hurled after us like missiles on the way home, wouldn't matter quite so much.

'I'm going to call him Peter,' I told Mum, who shrugged her shoulders and turned back to the sink. For once it didn't matter that she wasn't listening to me and that she wasn't interested in something I was excited about, because I don't think there's anything anyone could have said or done at that moment that would have dampened my pleasure. I felt as though I knew at last exactly what it must be like to be given a birthday present – but I was certain that none of my friends in London had ever had a present as wonderful as a rabbit.

I know it probably seems melodramatic to say that everything in my life changed from that moment, but it's true, because suddenly it had a positive focus. Every day when I got home from school, the first thing I did was go into the kitchen, lift Peter out of his hutch and stroke his soft, silky fur while I held his little body against my cheek and whispered to him all the things I had no one else to tell.

Then, one day, when I ran into the kitchen and knelt down in front of the hutch, it was empty. Mum had followed me into the room and was standing beside the stove, stirring something in a pan so that the air was filled with the strong, sweet smell of Indian spices. When I asked her, 'Where's Peter?' she didn't turn round as she answered, 'We gave him away. To someone who really wanted him.' Her voice sounded muffled and odd and when I jumped to my feet and burst into tears, I saw her flinch.

'What do you mean?' I shouted at her. 'I don't under-stand what you mean. *I* really want him. So why would you give him away? You know I love him. He's the only thing I've got that's mine. You told me that as long as I fed him every day and cleaned his cage, I could keep him. That's what you said! And I *have* looked after him! I don't understand, Mum.'

I was sobbing and the words were tumbling out of me in a torrent of distress, but my mother didn't look at me. And that's when a horrible, half-formed thought entered my head that made my heart beat fast and the palms of my hands start to sweat.

'*Why* did you give him away?' I yelled at Mum through my tears. 'Why won't you tell me what's happened to Peter? It's *him*, isn't it? *He's* done something to my rabbit.'

At that moment, Hassan walked into the kitchen and snarled at me, 'What's the matter with you? Why are you making all this fuss? It's only a fucking rabbit. It made too much mess. That's why we got rid of it.'

'We'll get you another one someday,' my mother mumbled, wiping the back of one of her hands across her cheeks.

I looked at her, not really understanding what she'd said, because the swirling mass of fog that had filled my head was making me feel dizzy and sick. And then I shouted at her, 'I don't *want* another one, I want *that* one. I want Peter.'

I ran out of the kitchen and up the stairs to my bedroom, where I threw myself, face down, on to my bed. I was still lying there, sobbing into my pillow, when Sami tiptoed into the room, laid his hand very gently on my shoulder and told me, 'He says you must come down and eat your dinner.'

That evening, Mum didn't sit at the table with us to eat the biriyani she'd cooked before we got home from school. It was chicken, and we almost never had enough money to buy chicken – or meat of any kind. But Mum said she wasn't hungry, and even Hassan's sharp, angry words couldn't make her change her mind. When Sami complained that the chicken tasted odd, Hassan slapped his face so hard that he knocked him out of his chair and sent him sprawling across the floor. For a moment, Sami sat there, dazed, with blood trickling out of his nose. Then he stood up, picked up his chair and as he sat down again, Hassan shouted at him, 'Just shut up and eat your fucking dinner.'

When Hassan turned to look at me, he seemed to be smiling, and that's when the terrible, unbelievable suspicion that had crept into my mind became a conviction.

I looked at my mother, who bit her lip and turned away, and then I stared at the food on my plate and retched, just as Hassan leaned towards me across the table, raised his hand as if he was going to strike me too, and yelled, 'Fucking eat it!' But I couldn't swallow.

When I ran upstairs to the bathroom to be sick, I saw what looked like spots of blood on the wall and a tiny clump of white fur in the plughole of the bath.

Even with the evidence staring me in the face, I couldn't believe that Mum would have let Hassan kill my pet rabbit. I knew she was frightened of him and that no one could really stop him doing whatever he wanted to do, but surely she could have found *some* way to stop him killing Peter? And even if she couldn't, she should have refused to cook my rabbit and let me eat him.

I felt sick and guilty. I was still crying when I confronted Mum later that evening, demanding to know the truth, and she told me, 'I *had* to do it.' She was clearly distressed and I was only seven years old, but I knew that there were some things no one would *ever* be able to make *me* do.

Maybe Hassan killed my rabbit because he was tired of eating meatless curries and watery soups. Or maybe he did it simply to be cruel, to show me who was in charge and what he was capable of. Whatever his reason for doing what he did, it had a devastating effect on me and I hated him for it. I couldn't have put it into words at the time, but I think it made me feel that there was never going to be anything good in my life again. And

I continued to feel guilty too, because I believed that if Mum hadn't got Peter for me and if I hadn't loved him, Hassan wouldn't have killed him.

Like most bullies, Hassan treated all animals with casual cruelty. So I was amazed when he came home some months later with a dog. It was a little sandy-coloured terrier that wagged its tail and looked up at us with big, anxious, brown eyes, and as soon as I saw it I wanted to scoop it up into my arms and cuddle it. But I hung back, afraid to show that I was interested in the little dog before I knew *why* Hassan had brought it into our house.

'I got it to cheer you up,' he told Sami and me and, when we hesitated to take the lead from his outstretched hand, he said, 'Well, go on, *take* it.' I reached out for it but as I did so, he snatched it back again and asked, 'Or don't you want him? I can take him away and give him to someone else if you don't want him.'

'He's beautiful. Of course we want him, don't we, Sami?' I said, closing my fingers tightly around the lead. I bent to pick up the little dog and buried my face in the fur on his neck so that my voice sounded muffled.

When Sami and I ran into the kitchen to show the dog to Mum, she seemed to like him, too. Although she grumbled about how much it would cost to feed him, she stroked his head and didn't click her tongue, as she always did when she was annoyed. So we kept him.

When I asked Hassan where the little dog had come from, he told me he'd bought him from a pet shop, which made me think that perhaps he did like us after all, because you'd *have* to like someone to buy them a dog, particularly when you had almost no money to spend on anything.

I tried not to think about Peter, because it made me so miserable when I did, but I never forgot about him, and the memory of what had happened to him made me wary about loving the little dog. But you can't really control something like that, and Sami, Asha and I *did* love him. We called him Boot, because he had one black foot, and we spent hours upstairs in the bedroom I shared with Asha, grooming him and trying to teach him tricks – without much success.

One thing that Boot *did* learn quickly was to stay out of Hassan's way – or at least beyond the reach of the toe of his shoe. Hassan didn't seek him out to hurt him, but he treated him the way he treated Sami, Asha and me – lashing out violently at him whenever he was in a bad mood.

One day, when we'd had Boot for about eight months, the little dog followed Hassan out of the garden when he was leaving the house, and Hassan suddenly turned around and started kicking him viciously. As Boot yelped in pain and tried to dodge out of the way, it was as if seeing the terrified little creature cowering there in front of him made something snap inside Hassan, and he couldn't control his fury. Boot was cringing against the fence beside the pavement and Hassan was drawing back his leg, getting ready to let fly one last massive kick, when an elderly lady almost ran across the road towards them.

Standing between Hassan and the dog, her whole body shaking with furious indignation, the woman shouted, 'You should be ashamed of yourself! What a terrible way to treat an animal, not to mention the distress you're causing to your poor children. I shall report you for what you were doing to that dog.' Then she bent down, scooped Boot up into her arms and marched off with him down the road, her anger so clearly apparent in the rigid straightness of her back that Hassan made no attempt to stop her.

Sami, Asha and I were devastated at losing Boot and I really missed him. Deep down inside me, however, I couldn't help feeling something very close to relief when I imagined the little dog in his new home – perhaps he was living with the old lady who'd rescued him – where no one ever hurt him or made him whimper with fear the way Hassan had so often done.

Years later, I told Mum that I sometimes used to wonder if the fact that Hassan had bought us a dog meant that maybe, on some level, he *did* like us. She laughed and said, 'Oh, he didn't *buy* that dog; he stole it out of someone's garden.' I didn't know whether to be more shocked by the callous cruelty of what Hassan had done or by my mother's apparent indifference to it.

After we'd been in Manchester for a while, Mum started supplementing the state benefits she was receiving by doing sewing again, and eventually she saved enough money to buy a second-hand car. It was old and very battered, and clouds of black smoke billowed out of its rusty exhaust pipe for as long as the engine was on, but just having a car at all allowed me to believe that things might not always be as hopeless as they'd been until then.

Despite having a car, we still didn't ever go anywhere. So on the day when Hassan told us he was taking us all to a farm, I could hardly contain my excitement. As I squeezed on to the back seat next to my brother and little sister, I remember thinking guiltily, *Perhaps he isn't a bad person after all. Perhaps he just gets cross and hits us because we're naughty, and he really does want to be a dad to us.*

Twenty minutes later, Hassan stopped the car on a patch of rough ground beside some low buildings made of rusty corrugated iron. Its wheels had barely stopped turning before I was trying to open the door beside me. Hassan turned off the engine, got out of the car and pushed the door closed again, trapping my wrist between the handle and the back seat. I cried out in pain and he bent down, put his head in through the open window and said, 'Just stay in the car.' Then he walked down the side of one of the buildings and disappeared.

So we sat in the car with Mum and waited until he reappeared around the corner of one of the sheds. He was accompanied by a man with a huge pot belly wearing dirty grey overalls that seemed to be several sizes too small for him. Hassan and the man were both carrying something in their hands, their arms stretched out in front of them, and at first I couldn't make out what it was. Then one of the poor creatures twisted its neck and squawked as it tried to flap its wings, and I realised that what they were holding were the legs of several scrawny, almost featherless chickens.

We all turned slowly in our seats to watch in silent

horror as Hassan walked round to the back of the car, kicked open the boot and dropped the chickens into it. Then, when the other man had done the same, he slammed the boot shut. Even when I pushed the tips of my fingers into my ears, I could still hear the horrible, panicked sound the terrified creatures were making.

Hassan said something to the other man and they both laughed. Then he got back into the driver's seat of the car, turned on the engine and pulled away from the side of the road without saying a word. And *we* didn't say anything either. Even Mum looked shaken, and I was so shocked that my mind seemed suddenly to have become completely blank, except for the image of those pathetically undernourished chickens being thrown into the boot in a heap on top of each other.

Hassan didn't speak to us on the way home. When I glanced up once and saw his face reflected in the rearview mirror, he was grinning, although his eyes looked cold and cruel.

When he stopped the car near our house, he told Sami to help him carry the chickens inside. As soon as Mum had lifted Asha out of her seat, I ran up the path behind her, desperate to get away in case he decided to make me help as well.

A few seconds later, there was an almost deafening

noise as Hassan and Sami walked in through the front door, leaving a thin trail of feathers in the air behind them. I could see that Sami was frightened by the squawking and by the way the chickens flapped and struggled in his hands, and it was only then that the full horror of what Hassan was going to do suddenly hit me.

I ran into the kitchen and pleaded with Mum, 'He's not going to kill them, is he, Mum? You won't let him kill them?' She just clicked her tongue and turned away from me, and I was sobbing as I fled into the back garden and covered my ears with my hands.

After that day, I felt sick every time Mum or Hassan opened the freezer and took out one of the plastic bags with a small, pale-coloured carcass inside it. And however angry Hassan was with me, I still refused to eat the chickens.

Hassan sometimes talked about his childhood growing up on a farm in a remote area in the hills of Morocco where, he told us, he'd worked hard every day from dawn till dusk since he was a small boy, and where life was harsher than anything we could possibly imagine. I could almost understand how growing up in a place like that, where you raised animals so that you had food to eat, might make you feel differently about them. But he *knew* that we loved animals and how upset we'd be, and he hadn't had to take us with him to buy those chickens.

At least his actions that day answered one question for me: Hassan *was* a bad person, and there was nothing he would ever be able to do that would make me trust him or think of him as my dad. However, it wasn't Hassan's deliberate cruelty or even his violent temper that was the worst thing about my life after he came to live with us. Even today, to be able to talk about some of the things he did to me, I have to pretend I'm describing things that happened to someone else.

For a while, Hassan didn't repeat what he'd done that first day: when he'd pulled me into Mum's bedroom and tried to force me to put my hand on his penis. But he did often press his body against mine and touch me in a creepy way when there was no one there to see what he was doing. He was sometimes almost nice to me while he was doing it, although he was instantly angry if I ever struggled and tried to get away from him.

After Hassan had come to live with us, Mum started cleaning the house, doing the washing and all the other household chores again, so at least his being there

meant that I was no longer going to school in dirty
clothes. After a while, however, he began to insist that
Sami, Asha and I should do all the cleaning and other
jobs around the house that we were capable of doing.
He didn't approve of us playing and messing around
like children normally do, and if I ever plucked up the
courage to ask, 'Can I go out to play, just for a few
minutes?' he'd shout 'No! Why do you need to play
outside? Just stay in the house.' Sometimes he'd be so
annoyed he'd smack me hard enough to knock me to
the ground and afterwards there'd be a ringing sound in
my ears.

Usually, Mum took Sami, Asha and me with her
whenever she went out, but the fact that we did all the
housework gave Hassan the perfect excuse to keep me
at home. He'd tell Mum, 'She can wash the dishes while
you're out,' or, 'Leave her here and she can clean the
kitchen floor.' And when Mum agreed, as she always
did, my heart would sink as I listened for the sound of
the front door closing, because I knew that as soon as
she'd left the house, Hassan would tell me to go upstairs
to their bedroom.

The first few times, he made me sit on the bed and
then he pulled my top over my head, dropped it on to
the floor amongst the damp towels that always littered

the carpet, and ran his short, thick fingers over my body in a way I didn't like. Then, one day, he told me to take off *all* my clothes and lie on the bed. I'd learned by that time that it was always best to do what he told me to do, but I felt frightened and, without thinking, I said, 'No! I don't want to do that.'

Instead of flying into a rage, Hassan just shrugged his shoulders, stood up and walked into the bathroom, which was in what was little more than a cupboard in the bedroom. After a few seconds, I stood up too I'd just put my hand on the handle of the bedroom door when Hassan called out to me from the bathroom, 'I thought you loved your brother. If you open that door, I'll know that you don't care what happens to him.'

I didn't understand what he meant, but the quietly threatening way he'd spoken made me stop. When I'd taken off my clothes and he was sitting on the bed beside me, running his hands over my child's body, I bit the inside of my cheeks to stop myself from crying.

A few days later, he did the same thing again, scratching my skin with his rough hands and then forcing them between my legs. A few days after that, he tried to kiss me. I didn't know what he was doing and, when he lowered his face towards mine and his foul, cigarette-breath filled my nostrils, I turned my head away. He gripped my chin tightly with his fingers, pulling my head back so violently that I felt a sharp pain in my neck, and then pushed his disgusting, wet tongue so far into my mouth that I began to retch.

For a moment I couldn't breathe and, as everything inside my head went black, I began to thrash around on the bed, trying to push him off me and crying, 'Don't! Don't do that. It's horrible. It makes me feel sick.' Instead of being angry, as I'd expected him to be, Hassan gave a bark of laughter, wiped his mouth with the back of his hand and said, 'Everyone does it. So you'd better get used to it.'

'I don't believe you,' I told him. 'I don't believe *anyone* does that. It's disgusting. I'm going to ask Mum if ...'

The saliva in my mouth tasted of stale cigarettes and I retched again when I swallowed it. As I did so, Hassan stood up, dug his fingers painfully into my shoulder until it felt as if they were bruising my bones, and said, very slowly, 'If you say anything to your mum, if you *ever* forget that this is our secret and you mustn't talk about it to anyone, I'll make sure you *and* your brother pay for it. Now put on your clothes and get out.'

He unlocked the bedroom door and, just as I was

running down the stairs, the front door burst open and Mum lifted the buggy into the hallway.

I stood on the bottom stair while Mum bent down to lift Asha out of the buggy. She glanced up at me and then straightened her back and looked at me again, more closely, as she asked, 'What's the matter with *you*? Why do you look as though you've done something wrong?'

I could feel the skin on my face start to burn and, for a split second, I imagined telling her what Hassan had just done to me, and what he did almost every time she went out and left me alone in the house with him. But even as the jumbled words began to form themselves into sentences in my head, I knew that I was far too frightened of Hassan ever to say them out loud. So I turned away from my mother and mumbled, 'It's nothing.' Then I walked slowly back up the stairs and into my bedroom.

Later that evening, after Asha had gone to bed and Mum, Hassan, Sami and I were sitting in the living room watching television, Hassan suddenly turned and shouted at Sami, 'Stop it! Stop making that noise!' Immediately my heart began to thud. I hadn't heard Sami make any sort of noise at all, and Mum obviously hadn't either, because she sounded as surprised and as anxious as I felt when she asked Hassan, 'What? What is it? What's he doing?' She looked at Sami and said, 'Are you making a noise? If you are, stop it.' And then, in the sort of placating tone of voice you might use to calm a fractious child, she told Hassan, 'He didn't mean it. He's sorry. He won't do it again.'

I knew that it was already too late to change the inevitable course of events and there was a sick feeling in my stomach as I watched Hassan's anger gather momentum until it finally erupted.

'Why does he have to breathe like that?' he bellowed, glaring at Sami with cold, narrowed eyes. 'Why can't he breathe quietly like other people?' As he said the last word, he reached across the sofa and hit Sami so hard on the side of his head that he knocked him, once again, out of his chair and on to the floor. When Hassan stood up, he towered above where Sami lay, curled up into a ball, his arms covering his head as he tried to protect himself against Hassan's next blow. But instead of hitting him again, Hassan began to kick his legs and stomach, shouting as he did so, 'Stop making that noise when you breathe. You don't need to breathe like that. You're just trying to wind me up.'

Mum fluttered around them, making darting movements with her hands as if she was trying to pluck up the courage to touch Hassan's arm and pull him away. All the time she kept saying, 'That's enough. Stop now. He won't do it again, will you, Sami? Stop. You'll hurt him. Let him get up now. Go, Sami! Go up to your room.' And when Hassan at last paused to draw breath, Sami managed to scramble to his feet and run out of the room.

I'd stood up too, when Hassan started kicking my brother, and as soon as Sami had gone, I edged my way towards the door. I'd almost reached it when Hassan turned so that his face was hidden from Mum's view, smiled a small, triumphant smile and mouthed silently at me, 'Next time, do what I say.'

Until that moment, I hadn't been able to think of any reason why he'd suddenly been so angry with Sami. But, of course, it wasn't Sami he was angry with. His fury had been completely contrived, because he wanted to send me a message and to let me know that what had just happened to Sami was *my* fault.

As I ran out of the living room and up the stairs, my heart was thumping in my chest and it felt as if cold liquid was flooding through my veins into every part of my body. After that night, I never complained or tried to wriggle free when Hassan touched me. If I *did* ever hesitate or show that I was reluctant to do what he wanted me to do, all he had to say was, 'If you don't do it, you'll be hurting your brother,' and I'd lie still, silently praying that Mum would come home soon, so that he'd unlock the bedroom door and let me go.

Chapter Five

EVEN IF NONE of us had ever done anything wrong at all, Hassan would still have found reasons to punish us and to vent the anger that seemed always to be building up inside him until it *had* to come out. It wasn't only because I was trying to protect Sami that I learned to do what Hassan told me to do: I also wanted to make things better for my mother.

Although I seldom saw Mum cry, she very often looked sad, and I felt that it was somehow *my* responsibility to make her happy – or, at least, not to give her any more reasons to be *un*happy. Hassan must have guessed how I felt, because if I did ever complain about what he was doing to me or threaten to tell Mum, he'd shake his head, sigh, and ask me if I was really so selfish that rather than do the one simple thing he wanted me to do, I'd prefer to upset her and cause her even more worry and distress. So I'd tell myself that I had to be brave for Mum's sake and not ever tell her what Hassan called '*our* secret'.

As the weeks passed, perhaps Hassan became more confident about Mum's apparent total lack of suspicion, as he stopped always waiting for her to go out before he did things to me. Sometimes, when she was in the kitchen making supper, he'd whisper to me to go up to their bedroom. I'd stand by the bed, listening to his heavy tread coming up the stairs, with a feeling inside me like a huge, trapped sigh that couldn't get out. Then he'd lock the bedroom door, open his trousers and say, 'Touch it. Go on. Hold it in your hand.' And I'd have to touch his horrible damp flesh with my fingers.

One day, when I was sitting on the bed and Hassan, naked, was moving his penis up and down in my hand, the handle on the bedroom door turned and then clicked back into place. Hassan leapt immediately to his feet and bent down to snatch up the towel he'd dropped on the floor beside the bed. As he wrapped it quickly around his body, he hissed at me, 'Stand up and keep quiet.'

I didn't understand the things he made me do to him, or the horrible things he did to me, but the fact that he didn't want my mother to know about them, and was so insistent that I didn't tell *anyone*, had already made me realise they were somehow 'wrong'. So as I stood beside my mother's bed with my heart crashing against my ribs, I felt as if *I* was the one who had a terrible secret that was just about to be discovered.

'Hello?' I could hear the bewilderment in Mum's voice. 'Are you in there?'

She turned the handle again, just as Hassan took two quick strides across the room, unlocked the door and pulled it open.

'Why was it locked?' Mum asked him. She moved her head as she spoke so that she could see around Hassan and into the room, to where I was standing nervously beside the bed. I thought I saw a wary, suspicious look flash across her face, but perhaps it was my imagination, born of guilt, because she sounded only annoyed when she snapped at me, 'What are you doing in here?'

My mind went completely blank and when I opened my mouth to answer her, I couldn't think of a single thing to say. And then Hassan answered for me.

'She's hiding from her brother,' he said, laughing and raising his eyebrows like an indulgent parent. 'They're playing a game.'

He smiled at Mum, but when he turned away from her to look at me, the expression on his face was threatening.

'Yes, I … I was hiding,' I stammered. As soon as I'd said the words, I knew that Mum would guess the truth – and then she'd be unhappy, Hassan would fly into a rage, and all the horrible things that followed would be *my* fault. And although the thought of what was about to happen made me feel sick, and I really didn't want Mum to be upset, I felt relieved too, because once she knew, she'd make Hassan stop.

Instead of confronting Hassan, however, my mother seemed to be angry with *me*: her voice was cold as she said, 'Get out of here. You shouldn't be in here.' As I ran through the open doorway, she reached out her hand and half pushed, half smacked me.

There were no raised voices from Mum's bedroom that night, and she never mentioned the incident again – or questioned me on the other occasions when she found me alone with Hassan behind a locked door. It must have required a huge amount of trust and naivety to accept what he told her, and I did sometimes wonder how she failed to notice my discomfort and distress. Perhaps she *did* suspect some-thing but didn't want to acknowledge to herself what Hassan might be doing. Or perhaps, as I've always wanted to believe, she really did have no idea about what was happening to me.

*

Hassan did become more cautious about touching me when Mum was in the house, but he continued to take me up to the bedroom almost every time she went out. I hated the things he did to me, but it was his violent rages that really controlled my life – and the lives of my brother and sister, too.

Days would sometimes pass without him losing his temper, and we'd begin to settle into an almost normal routine of daily life, although I still always felt that I was walking on eggshells around him, and I was terrified of doing anything that might annoy him and set him off again. Each time I was on the verge of wondering if he might really have found a way of controlling his anger, it would suddenly erupt again and he'd lash out and hit one of us with such force that he'd send us flying across the room, or he'd beat or kick my brother with such ferocity that Mum had to beg him to stop.

The problem was that while we had quickly become aware of some of the things that were guaranteed to trigger Hassan's fury, there were many others that no one could possibly have guessed at. In fact, it often seemed that a lot of the things that *appeared* to make him angry didn't really bother him at all: they were just the excuses he used so that he could release the rage that seemed to expand inside him like a physical entity.

Mum did most of the cooking at home, but she didn't know how to cook Moroccan food, and sometimes Hassan would make something himself. In the early days when we were living in Manchester, when Mum could rarely afford to buy meat, Hassan would occasionally cook horrible vegetable stews or – worst of all – disgusting soups, which he made out of a few vegetables and the water they were cooked in, together with some tinned tomatoes and peas. It didn't matter how revolting and unappetising his concoctions were, however: not eating your supper wasn't an option in our house.

Luckily, I've never been fussy about food and the only thing I really can't eat is okra; I can't understand why anyone would eat it willingly. Mum used to cook it in curries and, one day, when she served up a curry in which it was the main, repulsive, slimy ingredient, I told her, 'I don't want to eat it. You know I hate okra. Can I have something else?'

Suddenly, Hassan turned on me like a snarling dog and punched the side of my head with all his strength. As I lay on the floor, stunned and dabbing with the tips of my fingers at the blood that was trickling out of my mouth, he stood, towering above me, and bellowed, 'You'll eat what you're fucking given!'

I lifted up my arms to try to protect my head from his next blow but, at that moment, Mum appeared beside him and bent down to pull me to my feet, whispering as she did so, 'Go upstairs. Go! Quickly!' I cupped the palm of my hand underneath my throbbing jaw and ran out of the room and up the stairs to my bedroom, where I sat on my bed, still too stunned even to cry.

The unfairness of it all upset me almost as much as the fear and the physical pain, because I usually ate all the food that was given to me without complaining. It seemed that I wasn't allowed to have an opinion about anything, or certainly not one I dared to express.

I hated Hassan. I knew my dad wouldn't have hit me for saying I didn't like okra. In fact, Dad had *never* hit me like that for any reason, and I knew he never would. So why was Hassan allowed to do things to me that my own father wouldn't do? It wasn't right. And it wasn't right either that Mum was making us live the way we were living with Hassan. At that moment, I hated her too, because it was *her* fault that we'd come to Manchester in the first place, and it was only since we'd been living there that I'd been unhappy and afraid.

At last I began to cry, and I was still crying hot tears of frustration and hopelessness when Sami and Asha came upstairs. Asha sat down on my bed beside me and Sami sat on hers, his back against the wall and his face pale with anxiety. Asha touched my knee tentatively and asked me, 'Are you all right?' The fear I could hear in her voice made me sit up and wipe the tears off my face.

'Yes, I'm okay,' I reassured her. 'But it's not fair. He shouldn't be hitting us like that. He's not our dad. Mum shouldn't let him do it.'

I'd often complained to Mum about the way Hassan punished us, and about the injustice of her letting him hit us at all. When I said something to her the day after the incident with the okra, all she said was, 'Well, it's your own fault. If you kids are naughty, you're going to get smacked. You have to accept that. Everyone gets hit when they're naughty.'

'Not like that,' I told her – although, in fact, I didn't know if that was true. 'And anyway, we're not really naughty. Dad wouldn't ever have hit us like that, and he'd certainly never have beaten us the way Hassan beats us. And if Dad wouldn't do it, *he* shouldn't do it, either. If we're naughty and we deserve to be hit, *you* should do it.'

I knew Mum wasn't really listening to me, but she seemed to listen to Hassan when he said to her, 'They have to be taught to do what they're told. Why, when I was a boy I was beaten all the time. That's the trouble with kids in this country: they don't realise how easy they've got it.'

She accepted that he was right and that by punishing us so brutally, he was simply ensuring that we'd grow up to be obedient and respectful. So I was forced to accept it too, just as I had to accept everything else that was done to me when I was a child.

Even at that young age, I was aware that the things Hassan did to me weren't the paternalistic actions of someone who cared about my physical and emotional welfare. It seemed, however, that he really *was* concerned about the state of our souls.

As a Muslim priest, Hassan prayed five times every day, and he'd often berate Mum angrily because she wasn't bringing her children up to understand and practise the Muslim faith. And eventually, as she did with everything else Hassan wanted her to do, she gave in to the pressure he exerted on her and agreed that he could give Sami and me lessons in the Qur'an.

The lessons themselves didn't really make any difference to our lives – at least, not as far as curtailing any other activities we might have done, because we never played outside the house and rarely went anywhere except to school, to the local food shop and occasionally to the market when we needed new clothes. But I hated them. It wasn't that I minded having to learn the Qur'an, despite the fact that when you're just eight years old, trying to learn something you don't understand in a language you don't speak and can't read is a daunting and difficult task. What made me dread the weekly lessons was Hassan's anger whenever Sami or I made a mistake – which we did almost every time we opened our mouths.

As a good Muslim and a *mawlānā*, Hassan had learned the entire Qur'an by heart, which was what he expected us to do. Even though the Qur'an is written in Arabic – which was Hassan's native language – learning the *whole* thing was still a very impressive achievement. But Sami and I didn't speak or read Arabic, so we were going to have to learn it parrot fashion – verse by verse – without knowing what we were trying to say.

'You don't *have* to understand it,' Hassan would shout at us every time we made a mistake or complained that what he was expecting us to do was impossible. 'There are many people who speak Arabic who don't understand it. You just have to learn it. Now, say it again.' And he'd stand behind us as we stumbled our way through the verses he set us to learn at the end of each lesson, slapping our heads when our minds went blank or we mispronounced a word.

Poor Sami must have hated those lessons even more than I did. He'd stutter and falter over every syllable, the tremor in his voice becoming more pronounced as he struggled to get his tongue around the strange sounds. And all the time Hassan would be standing behind him, literally breathing down his neck. I could almost see the frustration bubbling up inside him until it exploded out of him and he'd hit the back of Sami's head and shout, 'You haven't even learned it!'

'I … I *have* learned it,' Sami would stammer. 'I j-just can't say the words.'

Hassan had no patience for our excuses and he'd hit Sami again and then bark at me, 'You say it!' And I'd try to catch hold of the letters and half-words that were flying around inside my head before Hassan reached out his hand to smack *me* and shout, 'You're not saying that right. I've told you a million times, it's a *hrgh* not a *huh*. Do it again. Do it properly.'

The lessons seemed to last forever, and all the time my heart would be thumping and I'd be longing for them to end. Finally, the moment would come when Hassan would stand in front of us, glaring like a belligerent bulldog, and say, 'Right, next time you must remember the whole verse, and if you don't recite it without any mistakes, there'll be *real* trouble.' Then Sami and I would almost run out of the room and up the stairs to our bedrooms, thankful that that day's lesson was over and already dreading the next one.

Despite the fact that Hassan's irritation and frustration during those lessons were almost palpable, he didn't ever lose his temper to the extent of doing more than smacking our heads – as I'm sure he would have done in any other situation. Even so, there was always a sick feeling in my stomach, the palms of my hands were always damp with sweat, and the certainty I felt that I would *never* be able to learn the verses of the Qur'an and that the lessons with Hassan would go on forever just added to the heavy weight of anxiety that had become an ever-present part of my life. And so, at first, I felt a huge sense of relief when Hassan announced one day that he wasn't going to waste his time on two such stupid children any longer and in future we'd learn the Qur'an at the mosque.

The following Wednesday, almost as soon as we'd got home from school, we left the house again to walk with Mum to the local mosque. There, Sami and I sat with the other hapless children, cross-legged in rows on the floor in front of beautiful, intricately carved lecterns made of scented wood, on each of which was an open copy of the Qur'an.

Whenever we made a mistake during the lesson our teacher slapped our hands. He didn't shout at us like Hassan did and I wasn't afraid of him, but I still hated it – not least because I knew I'd never be able to do what I was supposed to do. I was tired of trying really hard and never getting anything right.

After the first lesson at the mosque, I begged Mum, 'Please don't make me go again. What's the point of trying to learn something I can't understand? *You* don't know the Qur'an. You're not even a proper Muslim. So why are you making us learn it? It's only because *he* wants us to do it and you're trying to keep him happy. It's not fair.' Mum just clicked her tongue and didn't answer, and the next week she took us again, and the week after that.

It wasn't only the lessons themselves I hated; it was also the walk home from the mosque afterwards. We never went out of the house without Mum or Hassan, and whereas people rarely shouted abuse at us when Hassan was with us, they had no such qualms when we were alone with Mum.

One Wednesday evening, when we were walking

home after a lesson at the mosque, we passed a group of teenagers who were standing outside the local shop on the other side of the road. One of them called out something I didn't understand, and then they all began to chant, 'Paki, Paki, Bud Bud.' I was scared, as I always was when people shouted abuse at us, but this time I felt something else too, some other emotion that at first I didn't recognise. Then I realised it was *anger*. I was angry because the people abusing us were stupid, because they didn't know anything about us at all, and because it wasn't fair to make our lives even more miserable than they already were simply because we had brown skin and theirs was white. And then someone threw an egg, which hit me on the side of the head and exploded like a foul-smelling bomb all over my hair and face.

I was so shocked that I stopped walking, until I felt Mum tugging at my arm so that she was almost dragging me along the road beside her as she hurried towards the safety of home. Even home wasn't safe though, because Hassan would be waiting to test us on what we'd learned at the mosque, and to shout at us when we made a mistake. That night, as I stood in the bathroom trying to wash the stinking, slimy mess of raw egg out of my hair, I wondered how someone as religious as Hassan so clearly was could treat other people, even if they were only children, so harshly.

Eventually – maybe because of what happened on the way home that night – Mum seemed to give in to my pleading and she told Hassan, 'They'll learn the Qur'an when they're older.' He was angry and I heard them arguing long into that night, but Mum must have stood her ground for once, because the lessons stopped.

In the days between Hassan's outbursts of rage, when he was in a relatively good mood, he'd sometimes tell us stories about his childhood that I found intriguing – despite the fact that it was impossible to imagine him as a child at all.

'If I did anything wrong,' he'd say, 'my father would tie me by my ankles, hang me upside down from a tree and leave me there for hours.'

'Didn't your feet hurt?' I'd ask him. 'Didn't the rope cut into your ankles and make them bleed?'

He'd shrug his shoulders and say, 'That's just the way it was. If you did something wrong, you expected to pay for it. It didn't do *me* any harm. In fact, those punishments were the reason I'm as strong as I am today. I can take anything, because I had a tough upbringing.' Then he'd add proudly, 'That's what made me the man I am now.' And perhaps he was right.

Perhaps, too, it was at least partly because of the harshness of his own childhood that he was so critical and aggressive towards Sami, in particular. Hassan often sneered at us both and told us we were weak, but he was especially hard on Sami and he'd laugh nastily at him and tell him, 'You're a sissy. It's time you became a man. I worked on my family's farm – doing jobs that were back-breaking and exhausting – from the time I was a child far younger than you are now. I didn't snivel and complain, because I knew it had to be done. You're lucky by comparison. Your life is soft and easy. You need to toughen up and be strong. Why, even your sister is stronger than you are! Doesn't that make you ashamed?' It was what Dad sometimes used to say to Sami, but Hassan's criticism was coldly cruel and, unlike Dad had done, Hassan never did or said anything that might give any of us even a glimmer of hope that he cared about us. Each time he bullied and belittled Sami, I could see the hurt more clearly in my brother's eyes.

Despite sounding proud when he told us that the austerity of his own upbringing had done him no harm, I think Hassan had begun to realise that his anger was often completely out of proportion to whatever had given rise to it, and that he needed to learn to control his temper. Sometimes, after he'd beaten us or smashed up yet another television in a fit of rage, he'd say to Mum, 'I know I need to change.' But he never did.

At weekends when there was no school, Sami, Asha and I usually got up long before Mum and Hassan were awake, and we'd tiptoe downstairs to watch TV. We always thought we were being really quiet and so we were always taken by surprise when we heard Mum's or Hassan's angry voice shouting at us from upstairs to shut up. Then, one morning, we heard Hassan's heavy tread on the stairs and panic seemed to swell inside me as I searched frantically for the remote control.

'Switch it off!' I sobbed to my brother. 'Quickly, before he comes down.' But it was already too late. The door of the living room swung open and then crashed back against the wall, and the whole room seemed suddenly to be full of the energy of Hassan's fury.

Sami was standing at the end of the sofa when Hassan smacked him so hard that he fell on the floor. 'What the hell do you think you're doing?' Hassan bellowed at us. He reached out one hand and lifted me out of my seat by my hair, pulling me to my feet and then shoving me with all his strength so that I went sprawling across the coffee table, hitting my cheek and cracking my shin as I fell.

I was still lying there when he picked up the television, yanked its plug out of the socket on the wall, and slammed it down on the floor beside me. Hassan was still shouting as I scrambled to my feet and, pushing Asha ahead of me, ran up the stairs.

It wasn't the first time Mum had had to buy a television from a local second-hand shop to replace one Hassan had broken. But it wasn't only televisions he smashed. Sometimes, he'd swipe his arm across the mantelpiece, sending everything on it crashing to the floor, or hurl a heavy glass ashtray across the room – on one occasion missing Sami's head by only a fraction of an inch. I did sometimes wonder if he tried not to take his anger out on us – and I wondered, too, if one day he might end up killing one of us accidentally because he couldn't control his fury.

Between his rages, however, he'd be relatively calm for a few days – sometimes even for two or three weeks. But whether he was angry or in a good mood, he still took me upstairs and abused me almost every day. As he touched me and made me touch him, I tried to separate my mind from my body and think about the beating my brother wouldn't be getting that night because I'd done the horrible things Hassan had told me to do.

Mum and Hassan never took us anywhere, except

shopping, so Sami, Asha and I learned to entertain ourselves. We'd play together for hours. We were never bought any toys – except for the computer games Hassan sometimes brought home with him, which were really more for him than for us and which he smashed up regularly when he was in a temper. I didn't even have a doll or a teddy bear. For years, one of the things I wanted more than anything else in the world – almost as much as I wanted a birthday cake – was a Care Bear. I did eventually get one when I was in my teens and Mum bought me one at a car boot sale, by which time it was a bit late.

The only things we *did* have that were *almost* like toys were brightly coloured bedspreads decorated with pictures of rabbits and squirrels, and I'd often lie on my bed with my eyes tightly shut praying that the animals would come to life and play with us. While I waited for that to happen, Sami, Asha and I would sit on the beds in the room I shared with my sister and I'd make up stories about witches and goblins. Or Sami and I would describe the houses we were going to live in and all the things we were going to have when we grew up.

'I'll buy you a dog,' Sami used to say. 'Well, I'll buy you two,' I'd tell him. And sometimes I almost believed that the day might really come when we'd have the things we wanted and be happy.

I can't remember the order in which things happened at that time. Everything's jumbled up in my head and most of the things I *do* remember are like a series of flashbacks of events that aren't connected to each other along any sort of timeline. So I don't know how old I'd have been on the day that sticks in my mind as being the one happy day we spent together during the whole time we lived in Manchester. Maybe I was eight.

It was a lovely sunny day and, as I walked up the path to the front door when I got home from school, I could smell the strong, sweet smell of newly cut grass. Hassan was working in the back garden and when he saw us through the kitchen window, he called to us to go outside. My heart sank, and I crossed my fingers behind my back as I stepped out of the door. But, to my amazement, instead of berating us for something we'd done or failed to do, he began scooping up handfuls of grass cuttings and throwing them at us, laughing as he chased us around the garden. It wasn't a trick, as I thought at first it must be, and he continued to laugh when we threw the grass back at him and when we held each other by the ankles and had 'wheelbarrow races' across the lawn.

Hassan had never played games with us before; we hadn't ever had fun with him or enjoyed anything he'd been part of. Later that day, when I was sitting on my own watching television and he came into the living room, I told him, 'You know how you're always trying to get us to call you Dad, but I've never felt like I'm your daughter? Well, I feel really happy today and it's the first time I've felt as though you really are my dad.'

Hassan looked at me thoughtfully for a moment, then almost smiled as he said, 'Well then, we'll have to do things like that more often.' Of course, a couple of days later he was angry again and I felt stupid for believing that his light-hearted mood might last. Nothing good ever did.

Chapter Six

TO OTHER PEOPLE, Hassan may have seemed like just an ordinary man; in fact, some people probably thought he was a *good* man, because he'd taken on the role of father to another man's three children. They didn't see him when he was angry or being cruel or when he did something really nasty, apparently simply for the hell of it.

I was with him in the car one day when an old lady stepped off the pavement on to a crossing a little way up the road ahead of us. She clearly had difficulty walking and when Hassan first saw her he slowed down to give her time to cross the road. Then, as he got close to the crossing, he suddenly pressed his foot down hard on the accelerator and revved the engine. The old lady stopped and made a sort of staggering movement, and when she looked up at the car, there was an expression of pure terror on her face. I closed my eyes and cried out, because I knew we were going to hit her and I couldn't bear to see it happen.

Hassan just laughed and then, as I felt the car swerve, he shouted, like a nasty, spiteful child, 'That'll teach you!' When I opened my eyes again, I saw the old lady stumble and fall and as people rushed to help her, Hassan accelerated away. I don't know what happened to the old lady, or if she was badly hurt. I prayed for several days afterwards that she was all right.

I couldn't help wondering how Hassan would have reacted if someone had done the same thing to *his* mother. He didn't seem to care about anyone except himself, but I assumed he must love his own mother. And I suppose I believed that he loved my mother too – although I've never been able to understand why she loved him.

Mum must have been afraid of Hassan's rages: I can't believe anyone wouldn't have been. But she can't have been as frightened of him as we were, because she'd sometimes argue with him and I'd lie in bed at night with a sick feeling in my stomach, listening to them shouting at each other in their bedroom.

There were *some* things Hassan did that Mum didn't argue about, however – or even seem to question – despite the fact that they were very strange. Not long after Hassan moved in to live with us in Manchester, for example, Mum started having driving lessons. Her driving instructor was a woman Hassan had introduced to her and, sometimes, the woman would come into the house with Mum at the end of a lesson and, without saying a word to anyone, go upstairs with Hassan. They'd go into Mum's bedroom and close the door; then, an hour or so later, we'd hear the woman's footsteps on the stairs and the sound of the front door opening and closing again. Mum always had an odd expression on her face when she looked up from whatever she was doing to listen, but she never said anything, which I remember thinking even then was peculiar.

One day, I'd just walked out of the kitchen and into the hallway when the driving instructor ran down the stairs with her blouse only half tucked in and the zip on her skirt not properly done up. She looked agitated and her face was covered in red blotches, and she didn't seem to notice me as she fumbled with the catch on the front door. She slammed the door shut behind her as she left the house, and that was the last time I ever saw her.

What Hassan wanted at any particular time was the ruling factor in all our lives. There was never any choice about anything, for any of us: if Hassan told us to do something, we did it; and if he told us *not* to do something, we didn't.

Mum sometimes liked me to massage her feet while we were watching television in the evenings, and I liked doing it for her because she always said it made her relax. When I'd finished she'd sigh and say, 'Ah, that feels *much* better,' and I'd be pleased because I'd done something good for her.

The trouble with doing the massages was that it gave Hassan an excuse to make me do the same thing for him. But the soles of Hassan's feet weren't soft like Mum's; they were rough and calloused and covered in thick patches of dead skin, which he insisted on my removing with my fingernails. And because my fingers were only little, it made them ache, and I dreaded the times when he'd lie on the sofa and say, 'Can you massage *my* feet, too?' He always ignored me when I complained and would just say, 'Harder. Do it harder. Put some strength behind it.'

Worse than touching Hassan's feet, however, was having to massage his whole body. We'd all be watching television in the living room when he'd stretch his arms above his head and say to me, 'Go and make me some mint tea and bring it upstairs. My back aches and I need you to massage it.' I'd glance at Mum, willing her to say that I didn't have to go, but she didn't seem to think there was anything odd about his request at all. So I'd have to make the tea and carry it up the stairs to where Hassan would be waiting for me in their bedroom.

Sometimes, he *did* want a massage; more often he didn't. And even when I massaged him, he made me climb on top of him to do it and then touch him afterwards, so that I felt sick and anxious all the time because I was dreading what I knew was coming next.

One day when he told me to take a glass of tea up to the bedroom, something must have happened to give me the courage to say, 'All right, but I can't give you a massage today. My fingers hurt. Why don't you ask Mum to do it?'

Hassan stretched again and said, in a voice that to anyone else would have sounded perfectly normal, 'Because you're stronger than your mum. That's the only reason.' He shrugged his shoulders to show that he didn't really care one way or another, but it was clear from the expression on his face when he turned to look at me that he was angry.

Gradually, my memory of what our lives used to be like when we lived with Dad became so blurred that I simply accepted the new normality that had been imposed on us by Hassan – until one day, when I was almost twelve years old, he did something so terrible that I knew it wasn't 'normal' by any standard.

Hassan was good at DIY – it was the reason my father had wanted my mother to 'keep him happy' when he first became our lodger in London – and he decided to make a proper garden at the back of our council house in Manchester, with flower beds and a terrace where you could put a table and chairs. I liked helping him do DIY jobs, particularly when they involved gardening, so when he called Sami and me outside to mix some concrete, I went quite willingly.

I can still remember the look on Sami's face that day when he walked out of the back door and into the garden after Hassan had called us. It made me think of a dog that wants to take something someone's holding out to it but doesn't know whether it can trust that person. I knew that, despite the way Hassan always treated him, Sami still hadn't quite given up hope that one day he'd do *something* that would make Hassan like him – because that was what he wanted more than anything else.

I was already stirring the concrete powder into a bucket of water when Sami came out of the back door. Hassan snatched the piece of wood out of my hand and held it out to him, saying, 'Take this. Your little sister shouldn't be mixing concrete. It's a job for a boy.'

'It's okay,' I said quickly, reaching out to try to take

the stick back from Hassan. 'I don't mind doing it. I like it. It isn't hard.'

What I said wasn't true in fact, because it had started to take every ounce of my strength to move the piece of wood through the increasingly viscous mixture. I was just trying to divert Hassan's attention away from Sami. And as soon as the words were out of my mouth I regretted saying them.

Hassan pushed me away with his elbow and, smiling nastily at Sami, said, 'Do you hear that? It isn't hard at all. So why don't you give it a try?' It was an order, not the suggestion it sounded like, and Sami bit his lip as he took the piece of wood out of Hassan's outstretched hand. Grasping it tightly in his long, slender fingers, he planted his feet firmly on either side of the bucket, took a deep breath and tensed the muscles in his shoulders. As he did so, I prayed silently and fervently that some miracle would occur that would enable him to stir the mixture as easily as if it had been a bucket full of water. But however hard Sami strained, the stick wouldn't move, and suddenly Hassan shouted, 'You're fucking useless!' Sami winced and dropped the piece of wood on the ground. As he stumbled backwards, away from the bucket, Hassan almost screamed at him, 'You're worse than a fucking girl!'

I didn't see Hassan pick up the old, nail-studded floorboard that was in his hands when he started to hit my brother again and again, until the whole of Sami's body seemed to be covered in blood.

Once I began to scream, I couldn't stop. At first, Sami shouted too, and tried to protect himself against Hassan's blows by covering his head with his arms. But then he stopped making any noise at all and just lay on the ground, his body limp and unmoving, his eyes shut.

Hassan was still hitting him with the piece of wood when Mum came running out into the garden crying, 'No, no. Stop now. That's enough. You'll hurt him.' She grabbed Hassan's arm and held on to it until he dropped the blood-stained weapon at his feet and stood, breathing heavily, looking down at Sami's battered body.

Mum knelt on the ground beside Sami and tugged at his arm, saying, 'Get up now. You're all right. Get up, Sami.' Sami didn't move and I was suddenly certain that he was dead.

'You've killed him,' I shouted at Hassan. 'He didn't do anything wrong. It isn't his fault he isn't strong. You've killed him and I *hate* you.'

'Shut up.' Mum's voice cut across mine as she reached out her hand and slapped the side of my head. 'He isn't dead. He'll be all right. We just need to get him upstairs and put him to bed.'

Despite what she said, I could tell that she was really worried, and again I hated *her* too – for bringing Hassan into our lives in the first place and then for letting him hurt us. I wanted her to turn on him now and shout at him to get out of our house and never come back, but instead she told him, 'You'll have to carry Sami upstairs.'

At that moment, Sami opened his eyes, and I burst into tears of relief because he wasn't dead. But the way he stared straight ahead of him as if he couldn't see anything, and then closed his eyes again, made a cold shiver of fear run through my body.

'He's all right,' Hassan said. 'There's nothing wrong with him.' He shrugged as he bent down to lift Sami's unresponsive body off the ground and when I saw the look on his face, it made me wonder if he was afraid, as I was, that this time he'd gone too far.

None of us ever deserved to be punished the way Hassan often punished us; we never did anything really bad. In fact, he often beat us when we hadn't done anything at all, and although Mum would sometimes tell him to stop, she never *made* him stop. I couldn't ever understand why she didn't stand up for us, and now maybe it was too late and something terrible had happened to Sami.

When Hassan carried him up the stairs and dropped him on to his bed, Mum leant down and tried to pull the duvet out from under his body.

'Just leave him,' Hassan said angrily. 'He's all right. I barely touched him. He needs to learn to be a proper man. Leave him alone. He's fine.'

I was standing just outside the bedroom door, crying silently, when Mum spun around and said angrily, 'Stop snivelling and help me get your brother into bed.'

Grateful that there was something I could do for him, I dodged around Hassan as he strode out of the room and lifted Sami's legs further on to the bed so that Mum could cover him up.

Several times during that afternoon I stood in the doorway of my brother's bedroom, just watching him. He opened his eyes twice and made a low moaning sound, which caused the hairs on the back of my neck to stand up. Otherwise, he didn't move at all, and he gave no other signs of being conscious.

The next morning, when Asha and I woke up, we ran to Sami's bedroom. I knew as soon as we opened the door that something was seriously wrong. The first thing I noticed was the faint smell, a bit like stale or rotten food. When I pushed the door open further, I could see that Sami's body was twitching and that there was white froth bubbling out from between his lips and then being drawn back again into his mouth as he breathed.

As I crossed the landing and opened the door of Mum's bedroom, a voice in my head said, '*He's dying. Sami's dying.*'

'Mum,' I whispered loudly into the darkness. 'Mum, you've got to come. Sami's really ill.'

'Get out!' I could hear the anger in Hassan's muffled voice. 'What time is it? Why are you waking us up? Get out!' But Mum was already slipping her feet over the side of the bed.

I stood in the doorway of Sami's bedroom with my arm around Asha's shivering shoulders and watched as Mum shook Sami's arm, gently at first, and then more roughly.

'Wake up!' she said. 'Wake up, Sami. Can you hear me? Open your eyes.' Sami didn't move. When Mum pushed past us on her way out of the room, I could see the dread in her own eyes, and I could hear the fear in her voice as she told Hassan, 'We have to take him to the hospital. There's something really wrong with him. He's ...'

'No!' Hassan interrupted her; it sounded as though he was still in bed. 'I don't want to take him to the hospital. He doesn't need to go. And you'd better not take him either. There'll be trouble if you do.'

'We *have* to,' Mum insisted, and for once she sounded determined. 'I won't say anything. Just put him in the car. You don't need to come into the hospital with me.'

A few minutes later, Asha and I stood watching from the doorway of the living room as Hassan carried Sami down the stairs in his arms. 'There's nothing wrong with him,' Hassan told Mum again. 'I barely touched him. I didn't do anything to him that could have caused this.'

They lifted Sami on to the back seat of the car, and Asha and I stood on the doorstep and watched them drive away.

Later, when Mum and Hassan got back from the hospital – alone, without Sami – they were silent until they went upstairs, and then we could hear them shouting at each other behind the closed bedroom door.

The next day, I went with Mum to the hospital. I'd been really frightened by the way Sami looked when I'd seen him in bed the previous morning, but I was even more scared when I saw how pale he was now. He was lying on his back, perfectly still, his eyes shut, and there seemed to be tubes and wires connecting every part of his body to the sort of monitors and machines I'd previously only ever seen on the television. He looked small and frail and, despite appearing to be asleep, his face was set in an expression of anxious distress.

I began to cry, not only because I felt so sorry for him, but also because I felt guilty about what had happened to him. Perhaps the reason I felt guilty was because Hassan had instilled in me the belief that if I did what he told me to do, I could prevent really bad things happening to my family; so, therefore, if something bad *did* happen to one of them, it must be my fault.

I was still crying when a doctor came and stood beside us. He smiled at me and patted my shoulder, then he sighed and said to Mum, 'We still don't really know what's wrong with your son. So if there's *anything* you can think of that might be relevant, I hope you'll tell me.'

'I don't know what happened to him,' Mum said. 'He's very naughty. He goes out at night. I don't know what he does. I think he drinks.' She turned away from the bed and in a voice that was little more than a whisper, as if she didn't want Sami to hear what she was saying, she added, 'Maybe he was drinking and got into a fight. I found him like this in his bed in the morning.'

I couldn't take my eyes off Mum's face. I could feel myself blushing with shame for the glibness with which she was able to tell such terrible lies, and I felt angry too, because she was prepared to malign her own son rather than admit what Hassan had done to him. For almost five years, she'd been ignoring and overlooking the way Hassan treated us. Even so, I couldn't understand how she could bring herself to cover up for him after he'd beaten Sami so severely that he'd ended up almost comatose in hospital.

What was worse than that, however, was the fact that she was blaming *Sami*, making *him* out to be somehow culpable for what had happened to him, when the truth was that Sami *never* went out. At almost sixteen, he had no friends and was virtually a recluse. He'd always been shy, and moving schools so many times when we first arrived in Manchester – not to mention being afraid to leave the house because he knew he'd be chased down the street by thugs shouting racial abuse and throwing things at him – had made his social anxiety far worse than it might otherwise have been.

I must have made a noise, because the doctor turned and looked at me quizzically. As he did so, Mum took a step forward, rotating her shoulders slightly so that she was blocking me from his view, and said, 'She's upset.'

The moment had passed and I knew I wasn't going to say any of the things I wanted to say, which meant that Mum's lies about Sami would remain uncorrected and – most importantly of all – that Hassan would get away with having almost killed my brother for no reason other than because he had a vicious temper he couldn't, or wouldn't, control.

While Sami was in hospital, the doctors did a whole series of tests and examinations, but they still couldn't work out what was wrong with him. The plausible explanation Mum had given them for the bruises that covered his body didn't explain quite so well why he persistently refused to eat so that he had to be put on a drip, or why he lay in a hospital bed day after day and didn't speak. They still hadn't found any definitive answers by the time Sami was discharged from the hospital, two weeks after Hassan's vicious attack.

I was really excited at the thought of having Sami at home with us again. Mum kept saying, 'He'll get better; he just needs time,' but I knew almost immediately that he'd been damaged in some way that could never be put right. Even in the relatively short time he'd been in hospital he'd lost a lot of weight and, when he came home, he was so thin I imagined that if you held his arm too tightly, it would snap in half in your hand. Not that you *could* have held his arm, because he wouldn't allow anyone to touch him.

It seemed that the light inside him – which had never burned very brightly – had gone out entirely, and he'd become a different person. It didn't matter how many times Mum told us – almost as if she was trying to convince herself – that he'd be all right, I knew that part of Sami had gone forever. When he wasn't in bed, he was in the living room, sitting completely motionless on the sofa and staring at the television without appearing to focus on or understand what he was watching. It wasn't long before I realised that it was pointless trying to get him to talk to me. So I'd just sit beside him when I came home from school, keeping him company while he watched television and feeling inordinately pleased whenever he *did* say anything to me, even if it was only to ask me to get him a glass of water from the kitchen.

No one seemed to know what was wrong with him. Although they'd said at the hospital that, physically, he seemed to be okay, it was clear that *something* was wrong, because he'd become little more than a zombie: he was so disengaged from everything that was going on around him that nothing seemed to penetrate the apparently empty world into which he'd retreated.

As the days passed and he still didn't get any better, I kept trying to think of something I could do that might bring the old Sami back again. But, in the end, it wasn't me who came up with a plan.

'He's possessed by *jinns*,' Hassan told Mum one day.

Mum had lots of superstitions and, while I doubted most of them, I did know that, according to Islamic teaching and Arab folklore, *jinns* are spirits that get inside people and make them do things they wouldn't normally do. Despite her beliefs, however, Mum looked sceptical.

'That's why Sami's behaving like this,' Hassan persisted. 'It's a *jinn*, I'm certain of it. I barely touched him. Nothing I did could have caused him to be like this. It's the only explanation.'

'Well …' Mum still hesitated, but I could see that she was wavering. 'I don't know,' she said at last. 'I think we should wait and give him time to get better. He doesn't look as pale as he did when he came home from the hospital. So we'll give him more time. That's the best thing to do.'

'He's already had enough time,' Hassan said. 'I'm sick of seeing him sitting there on the sofa like some stuffed animal. I didn't hurt him. A *jinn* is causing this and we need to get it out of him. Look at him. He can't even walk properly and he isn't eating; he just sits there all day, and it's getting on my nerves.'

Mum continued to resist for a while, but eventually agreed — as she always did to anything Hassan had set his mind on — and told him, 'Well, if the doctors can't fix him, perhaps you're right and the *mawlānās* can.' So a date was set when two of Hassan's friends would come to the house to perform a ceremony to banish the spirits from poor Sami's already beleaguered and exhausted body.

I begged Mum not to let them do it. 'Sami's ill,' I told her. 'Hassan beat him with a plank of wood that had nails in it. *That's* what made him like this. It isn't evil spirits. That's ridiculous and you know it is. Please, please Mum, don't let Hassan do this. Don't trust him. You don't even know what they're going to do. Please. Sami's been through enough. You said yourself that he just needs to rest.'

But Mum had made up her mind and she refused to listen to me. Once she'd accepted that Hassan was going to do whatever he thought fit, she seemed to embrace the idea of the ceremony wholeheartedly, brushing aside my increasingly desperate pleas and focusing her mind on the day when the evil spirits would be driven out of Sami's body and he'd be well again.

'He knows the Qur'an 100 per cent,' she told me impatiently. 'He knows all about *jinns*. He'll get them out of Sami. In any case, the doctors weren't able to cure him, so there's no harm in trying.'

My mother has always been good at believing whatever suits her purposes at the time, but I couldn't understand how she'd managed to convince herself that Hassan wasn't responsible for Sami's illness: I'm certain she knew in her heart that he was. Maybe she *did* believe that Sami was possessed by evil spirits, or maybe she was giving Hassan the chance to mend what he'd come so close to destroying. Whatever her reasons, however, I don't suppose she could have known how much more damage Hassan and his fellow *mawlānās* would do.

On the day when the ceremony was due to take place, Mum spent the morning in the kitchen making little cakes and laying them out carefully on brightly coloured dishes. Then, while she cleaned the living room, Asha and I put sticks of incense into pots and lit them, so that by the time the *mawlānās* arrived, the house was filled with a strong, sweet fragrance. It made me sad, because it reminded me of all the religious festivals we'd celebrated with our family in London.

Hassan took the two men into the living room and

Asha and I stood just outside the door, watching them silently as they opened the bags they'd brought with them and laid out all the paraphernalia of their beliefs on the coffee table.

Sami had stayed upstairs in his room all morning, but when the men arrived, Hassan went up and brought him down. As Sami walked nervously and clearly reluctantly ahead of Hassan into the living room, I caught a glimpse of his pale face and heard him whisper to Hassan, 'What are you going to do? I don't want you to do this.' And then Hassan closed the door.

After a few minutes, Mum came out of the kitchen and stood with Asha and me in the hallway, listening to the low murmur of the men's voices. I had no idea what was involved in getting *jinns* out of people's bodies, but some instinct told me that it wasn't something you'd want to happen to someone you loved. I'd begged Mum earlier that day not to let Hassan perform the ceremony on Sami, and she'd been impatient with me and told me it was 'just a ceremony'. But I could tell from the expression on her face now, and from the way she was clasping her hands tightly in front of her, that she was anxious too, and not nearly as confident as she'd pretended to be.

So my stomach was already churning when we heard

Sami shout, 'No! Stop! You're hurting me. Stop it, please.' Despite his voice being slightly muffled, there was no mistaking the sound of his fear and my heart was thudding as I glanced at Mum, expecting her to open the door and tell Hassan to stop. But she didn't move, and when I whispered urgently to her, 'Mum, please stop them; they're hurting him,' she just waved her hand as if she was brushing away a fly.

A few seconds later, Sami cried out again, and this time he sounded as though he was on the verge of full-blown panic as he pleaded, 'Get off! Get off me! Nothing's happening. I've told you. It isn't working. I can't breathe. Stop it! *Please.*'

Asha began to sob and, as I put my arm around her shoulders, I started to cry, too. And finally Mum did turn to look at us, only to hiss angrily, 'Go upstairs! Go! Go away!' I don't think she was really angry: I think she was as upset as we were, and her impatience was simply an attempt to cover it up. So perhaps she was as frightened as we were as we ran up the stairs to our bedroom, and maybe she felt as guilty as I did when I closed the door because I couldn't bear to hear the sound of Sami's terrified screams.

For what seemed like hours, Asha and I sat on my bed with our arms wrapped tightly around each other. I tried to think up stories to tell her, to take our minds off what was happening to our brother until, eventually, the men left. We waited a few minutes and then went downstairs, by which time Sami had already shut himself in his bedroom. He refused to come out or to speak to me when I stood beside his bed and whispered that I was sorry about what they'd done to him and that I loved him.

When he did leave his room the next day – because Hassan insisted that he did – nothing had changed, except that Sami seemed to have withdrawn even deeper into the silent, unhappy, lonely world he'd inhabited since the day Hassan had beaten him so badly. He sat on the sofa in the living room, just as he'd done before, and when Mum asked, in a voice so quiet that I wondered if she'd been crying, if he wanted anything to eat, he looked directly into her eyes and said, 'I'm not possessed by an evil spirit, Mum. You know I'm not. So why did you let them do that to me?'

Mum didn't answer. When I asked her the same question later, she told me, 'Well, he would say that, wouldn't he?' Then she turned away from me and refused to talk about it again.

After what happened that day, I couldn't believe it when Mum let the *mawlānās* come again, and it wasn't until after their third visit that she told Hassan she wanted them to stop. 'It isn't working,' she said. 'So perhaps Sami doesn't have a *jinn*. Perhaps he'll just get better on his own if we give him time.' And that's eventually what seemed to happen, although Hassan claimed that the ceremonies were really what had cured him. In reality, however, he hadn't been *cured* at all.

It was years later when Sami finally told me what Hassan and the other *mawlānās* had done to him: 'They forced sharp things under my fingernails,' he said, sobbing once and then speaking in a flat, emotionless voice, his eyes focused unblinkingly on something in the distance that I couldn't see. 'It hurt so much that I thought I was going to pass out. They wouldn't stop doing it. They were humming too, and then talking really fast, saying things I didn't understand so that it seemed that they were the ones possessed by spirits instead of me.

'They kept telling the *jinn* inside me to admit that it was there, and then they beat me. They said they had to do it to force the *jinn* to come out of my body, but I think it was really just an excuse for Hassan to hurt me again. Then they held me down and blew incense into my face until it filled my nostrils and my mouth so that I couldn't breathe and I thought I was going to die.

'They tried to make me drink something from one of their bottles, but it tasted disgusting and I thought they were trying to poison me. When I couldn't swallow it, they forced some of it into my mouth and even though it made me retch, they held me down on the sofa and poured it down my throat until I choked.'

I cried as Sami described what had happened to him that day, and I wondered yet again how our mother could have stood outside the living-room door listening to the sound of her own son's screams, and done nothing to stop what Hassan and his friends were doing to him.

Chapter Seven

WHEN I WAS twelve, my mother's father died and Mum, Sami, Asha and I went to India for his funeral. It was the first time I'd ever been there – or anywhere outside England – and I'd never met my grandfather or any of the other members of my mother's family except for my auntie, with whom Mum had come to England when she was thirteen. My mother's sister also went out to India for their father's funeral, but we barely saw her while we were there.

We were away for eight weeks. Because my mother and father were cousins, they had some distant relatives in common, but we stayed with members of Mum's immediate family and I loved spending time with them. Some people did criticise Mum and say that she was an outcast who had brought shame on her relatives by leaving my father. But because her brothers, my uncles, had clearly forgiven her for what had happened, no one dared to say anything openly, to her face, and the only hostility we were aware of was the gossip that was reported to Mum by her mother.

My uncles and their wives were kind to me, and my cousins put their arms around me, held my hands and made me feel like someone special. Even better than that was waking up every morning and remembering that Hassan wasn't there, and feeling as if someone was lifting a weight off my chest and untying the knot that had been constricting my stomach.

I don't know how I'd expected to feel about being in India, and I was surprised to find that being there made me feel very English. Everything seemed strange and I realised that I wasn't really Indian at all – at least, not in the way my mother was. I was twelve, but looked quite mature for my age – certainly older than most of the sixteen-year-old girls I met there – and the overt and sometimes intrusive interest I attracted made me feel very uncomfortable. It wasn't unfriendly in any way – and never aggressive – but, even so, I didn't like it.

When I was young and we used to get together with Mum's sister and her family and Dad's relatives in London, I always thought they must be the noisiest people in the whole world. However, the sounds and the colours and the smells that overwhelmed my senses as soon as we stepped out of the doors at the airport in India were completely beyond anything I could have imagined.

I realised almost immediately, as we and some of the relatives who'd come to meet us tried to squash ourselves into a taxi, that in India there's no such thing as personal space – in fact, there seemed to be very little space of any kind. The taxi driver was directing the operation from the pavement, which really just involved smiling an almost toothless smile and waving his arms in encouragement while I became pinned to my seat against the door of his taxi by hot, sweating, chattering bodies.

Eventually, when not even the tiniest, thinnest child in the world could have been shoehorned on to the back seat beside us, I turned towards the open window and found that I was looking directly into the face of a scrawny, wizened old man who was sitting on the seat of a bicycle-driven rickshaw.

The man was so close to me I could smell the sour smell of his breath and I gave a startled little cry and tried to move away from the window. But the car was packed so tightly with bodies that I could hardly turn my head and, when the old man reached out with his hot, lizard-skinned fingers and stroked my arm, I only just managed not to scream.

Fortunately, the taxi driver had already pressed his weight against the door on the other side of the car to force it shut, climbed in behind the wheel and started the engine and as he glanced in his broken mirror and the car pulled away from the curb, the old man withdrew his hand.

My first impressions of the dusty town where my mother's relatives lived were that it was overcrowded and poor. There was little to like about the town itself, but the people we met there were lovely. They all seemed to talk at the same time, very loudly and in a language they spoke so quickly I could barely understand anything they said. For a child who'd never been cuddled and who'd had virtually no loving physical contact from any adult, what struck me most about my relatives was the way they threw their arms around me and hugged me so tightly they almost squeezed all the air out of my body. They did it often, and sometimes without any apparent reason, and it made me feel that I belonged to them and they loved me.

My mother's mother was different, however, and after meeting her I realised why Mum didn't ever kiss and cuddle us in the way I'd always longed for her to do. Mum was one of five siblings, three of whom were boys, and although my grandmother fawned over her sons, she seemed almost indifferent to her daughters. In contrast to almost everyone else we met in India, my mother's mother didn't once hug or even put her arms around the daughter she hadn't seen for so long.

The noise in India was extraordinary. It was constant – made by the people, the dogs that wandered loose in the streets and the finches that lived in cages on the open balconies of almost every house. At six o'clock every evening, even the sound of the finches was drowned out by the almost deafening screeching of the parrots that flew overhead in their hundreds in swirling clouds of bright, iridescent colour, and then, an hour later, by the high-pitched squeaks of the bats that swooped and soared around the low roofs of the houses.

My mother's father had been quite well off – particularly in contrast to the poverty of most of their friends and neighbours – and the rickety old motorbikes that belonged to two of Mum's brothers were considered locally to be pretty impressive. Fortunately, we travelled everywhere in taxis or rickshaws while we were there; even then we were dicing with death, because everyone seemed to drive as if they were taking part in a race, which would have been frightening enough even if the roads hadn't been strewn with rocks and full of deep pot holes.

Our relatives in India thought we were rich, which I suppose we were by comparison, and I could see that Mum enjoyed being the object of their envy as she gave them gifts of the clothes we'd grown out of and, to one of her brothers, a watch that for some reason Sami would no longer wear. But it wasn't their admiration that made our visit such a good experience for *me*; it was the feeling of being liked and accepted by everyone I met there.

There were things I didn't like about the town where our relatives lived: apart from taking your life in your hands every time you travelled anywhere by road, I never got over the embarrassment of having to go to the loo in a pot or in a hole in the ground, and I hated the casual cruelty with which many people treated animals. Even so, I *loved* being there and I don't think I met a single person I didn't like. Every day felt like a holiday and I dreaded the thought of having to go home – not least because I knew that when we got there, Hassan would be waiting for me.

I think Mum's relatives were hoping that Sami or I would fall in love with one of their children so that they would be able to go to England like Mum had done and have all the advantages and benefits she boasted about having in her life there. I know that they were very keen for me to like a particular cousin, who was a boy of about sixteen. And I *did* like him, although at the age of twelve the idea of marrying *anyone* was just embarrassing.

Not everything was perfect while we were there, however, and I was constantly struggling to suppress two particular anxieties. One was the fear that my relatives would realise that I was 'dirty' – as Hassan often told me I was when he rubbed his body against mine – and then they wouldn't like me any more; and the other was that I was very ill and was going to die.

Before we'd left England, I'd been getting ready to go to bed one night when I'd noticed what looked like spots of blood in my knickers. I'd rushed into the bathroom and wiped myself with toilet paper, and immediately the blood was there again. Clearly, I was bleeding from *inside*. I knew something must be really badly wrong with me, and I was very relieved when it stopped after a couple of days. But then, a few days later, it had started again, and that time I'd had a terrible tummy ache, too.

I'd sat down on the edge of the bath and begun to cry. It wasn't fair. Although I'd stopped being a happy child shortly after we'd moved to Manchester, I didn't want to die. What also upset me was the thought that when I did die, my mother would be sad, and then all the times I'd been brave for her sake would be erased, because I'd have ended up making her unhappy after all.

There hadn't been any more blood after that day – until we'd been in India for a couple of weeks and it started again, and this time it wasn't just a few spots: I'd gone to the toilet one morning and my knickers had been soaked in it. I'd heard about people bleeding to death, and suddenly I knew that that was what was going to happen to me.

I tried to console myself with the thought that at least if I died in India, where Mum was with her family and the people who really cared about her, it wouldn't be as bad as dying at home in England, where there'd only be Hassan to look after her, and where I didn't think anyone at all except Asha, Mum and perhaps Sami would mourn for me.

Later that morning, I sat on the sofa in the house belonging to one of my uncles and aunts and tried to focus on what people were talking about. I was sure that I could feel blood seeping through the thin cotton fabric of my favourite Asian suit and I didn't dare stand up in case everyone saw it. Even after they all went out to look at something my aunt wanted to show them in the garden, I made some excuse and continued to sit there for as long as I could, until I was bursting to go to the toilet.

When I stood up and saw the dark stain on the sofa, I thought I was going to die of shame. Just at that moment, my aunt came into the room and saw it too.

'Aren't you wearing a sanitary pad?' Auntie exclaimed. 'Have you run out of them? Why didn't you say anything?'

'I ... I don't know what's wrong with me,' I stammered, hot tears of humiliation and self-pity streaming down my cheeks. 'Please, Auntie, don't tell Mum. She's got enough to worry about already without this. Don't tell her that I'm dying.'

'Dying?' My aunt looked baffled, and then she clapped her hands in dismay as understanding dawned on her. 'You've got your period, child,' she told me. 'You're not dying. There's nothing *wrong* with you. Hasn't your mother told you about it?' And when I began to sob, she put her arms around me and said, 'Why, you poor child! That mother of yours is hopeless.' And then she explained to me about periods, showed me how to use a sanitary pad and gave me one of my cousin's saris to wear while she washed the blood out of my clothes.

I don't know if my auntie ever managed to get the stain out of her sofa: to my amazement, she was far more concerned for me than she was about the possibly irrevocable damage that had been done to her furniture. And I think it was the sympathy she and my cousins so clearly felt for me that made me wonder, for the first time, if I wasn't really to blame for all the bad things that happened in my life. Perhaps I wasn't evil, as Hassan always told me I was; maybe it wasn't *my* fault that Mum was unhappy; and maybe it wasn't entirely my responsibility to try to make her feel better about her life.

When we were in India, I became consciously aware for the first time that not all mothers were like mine, and I began to wish that Mum could be more like my auntie. I'd already realised that she was naïve and that there were a lot of things in life she didn't understand. But that didn't explain why she didn't tell me about the things she *did* understand – like periods and, when I was younger, washing your clothes so that you don't go to school reeking of body odour.

For as long as I could remember, it had always felt as if Mum didn't really care about me, or about Sami or Asha. She didn't protect us against Hassan's physical assaults, and she didn't even seem to notice any of the signs – which I realised much later *must* have been there – that he was sexually abusing me. Mum didn't seem to see us, and I'd learned to lock up all my emotions deep inside me and try to accept the way she was.

It turned out that I wasn't dying after all, but it began to become clear that there was something quite seriously wrong with Sami. He'd started behaving oddly before we left England, and while we were in India it got worse. He didn't do anything terrible; he just did things that made people laugh at him. Mum kept insisting that it was because he was finding it difficult to cope with the heat, and it was true that it was incredibly hot: it was as if you were surrounded all the time by a solid but invisible wall of heat that you could have reached out and touched with your hand. So the first time Sami walked out naked on to the open verandah of the house where we were staying, it was just about plausible to explain his behaviour as a heat-related aberration.

The next day, when he stepped off the verandah and walked down the street without any clothes on and my uncle had to run after him and try to persuade him to wrap a piece of material around his waist, Mum's explanation began to seem a bit less likely.

A few days later, I was inside the house when I heard

the sound of people laughing. It seemed to be coming from the narrow lane between our house and the neighbour's. When I went out on to the verandah, I could see Sami standing in the garden. Again, he had no clothes on. He was holding the end of a garden hose against his body as if it was an extension of his penis, giggling like a child and calling out to the little group of people who'd gathered to watch him, 'Look! Look at this!'

'It isn't funny,' I snapped at him, jumping down from the verandah and snatching the hose from his hand. Then I touched his arm more gently and said, 'Come inside, Sami. You must put on some clothes. Everyone's laughing at you.'

He turned and looked at me, apparently without recognising me. Then he shook my hand off his arm, pushed me roughly away from him and shouted, 'Leave me alone. Don't touch me. If you touch me again, I'll bock you.'

'Bock me?' I repeated. 'What does that mean? You're not making any sense! *Please*, Sami, come inside. I hate to see people laughing at you.'

But his mood had already changed again and he held his hand over his mouth and giggled. When I looked into his eyes, it was like looking through a window into a dark, empty room.

Later, when I told Mum what had happened, she said, 'Perhaps he's possessed again. It must be a *jinn* that's making him do these things.'

'No, I don't think it's a *jinn*,' I told her. And when she shrugged her shoulders and said, 'No, you're right,' I felt myself relax a little at the thought that she'd finally accepted the fact that Sami wasn't well. But my relief was short-lived. 'It's what I've been saying all along,' Mum continued. 'It's the heat. That's all it is. He'll be all right when we get back to England.'

I knew there wasn't any point arguing with her. I wished I could share her certainty – although I didn't know how certain she really was, because it was clear that she'd decided to ignore any of the facts that didn't fit with what she wanted to believe.

For the rest of the time we were in India, Sami's behaviour became increasingly bizarre until he was almost completely out of control. Eventually, even Mum had to face reality and accept that there was something seriously wrong with him: he'd often disappear from the house, and when Mum's brothers went out to search for him, they'd find him wandering the streets on his own, sometimes naked and always frightened, because he didn't know where he was or how he'd got there. Despite feeling ashamed and embarrassed when people laughed at him, I dreaded the thought of going home, where we wouldn't have Mum's family to support us and where no one would wrap their arms around me and tell me not to worry.

I wouldn't have been looking forward to going home even if Sami hadn't been behaving strangely and even if I hadn't dreaded the prospect of going back to live with Hassan. In the few weeks we'd been in India, I'd felt almost the way I used to feel when we lived with Dad – that I wasn't responsible for what happened in our lives, because there were other people there who could take care of things and make the decisions that needed to be made. And, even more importantly, I now knew what it was like to live with people who seemed to love me.

Someone had given us a cat a few weeks before we'd left England and I realised that seeing it again was the only thing I had to look forward to. But even that made me anxious, because I knew that there was a strong possibility that Hassan would have got rid of it, in one way or another, while I wasn't there to protect it.

I cried and cried when we left our relatives in India. I sat on the plane, looking out at the sky and praying that we'd arrive home to find the house empty and Hassan gone. If we didn't have to live under the shadow of Hassan's anger, there would be nothing to be afraid of all the time and I wouldn't have to keep secrets about things I didn't understand. Long before our plane began to descend through the clouds above London, the knot that hadn't tied itself around my stomach for eight weeks was already being pulled tight and, when we got home, Hassan was waiting for us.

I almost cried with relief when I saw the cat sitting on the bottom stair, licking his paws with an air of detached indifference, which was belied by the fact that when I scooped him up into my arms, he purred and pressed his head against my shoulder. Hassan had cleaned the house from top to bottom, whereas normally he never cleaned even the smallest part of it, and it seemed that he was pleased to see us too – or, at least, to see Mum. But it wasn't long before Mum went out and Hassan took me upstairs to their bedroom. A couple of days later, something happened to make him angry and he picked up the little table in the living room and smashed it down on the floor so that it broke into a dozen pieces. Suddenly, the love and the laughter we'd shared with our family in India seemed like a distant dream.

Mum turned out to be wrong about Sami: his strange behaviour didn't stop when we were at home again, and eventually she took him to the doctor, who referred him to the hospital for more tests. They still couldn't work out what was wrong with him, except to say that they were now pretty sure the problem was mental rather than physical, and Mum still insisted that his illness had been caused by the heat in India and had nothing whatsoever to do with the horrific beating Hassan had given him that day in the garden.

Chapter Eight

FOR A LONG time after Mum left Dad, he kept hoping that she might go back to him. He didn't seem to care about the terrible shame she'd brought on him – as well as on herself and both their families. Some people saw what had happened as a reflection of weakness in Dad, which made him unable to control his wife. It must have been very hard for him, and he must have loved Mum to have been prepared to have her back.

Until Mum left him, he'd had a lot to be proud of. He'd been doing everything the Indian way: he'd married his cousin, who he'd brought over from India; his wife had born him children – most importantly, a son; he'd worked hard and bought a house, and then another, which he'd let out to tenants; and he'd been living a respectable life in the heart of a Muslim community, surrounded by his family.

After Mum ran off with Hassan, however, people began to ask, often quite openly, 'What sort of man allows his wife to be snatched away from right underneath his nose? He must be simple to have left that lodger alone in his house with his pretty young wife and not even to have suspected what was happening.'

They also derided Dad for allowing Mum to take his money, because when he finally accepted that she wasn't going to go back to him and they were divorced, the house in London that she was awarded in the divorce settlement was the one that had been paid for, while Dad was left with the one on which there was still a hefty mortgage owing. In fact, it wasn't long before he lost that house, too, because he couldn't meet the repayments.

People, including Mum, used to say Dad was slow-witted – 'not the sharpest tool in the box'. I think it was just that he was like Sami used to be as a child, before he became ill – unaggressive almost to a fault and trusting to the point of naivety.

After my parents had divorced, Hassan kept pushing Mum to marry him, but she always found an excuse not to. He wanted a British passport, which I've always assumed was at least part of the reason why he was keen to get married. Mum was already supporting him, and

I think it was because she knew that if she *did* marry him, he'd be entitled to half of whatever she owned that she was reluctant to do so. 'The money's for the kids; I've got to look after them,' she'd tell him, which was ironic, considering she did almost nothing to look after us in the ways that really mattered.

In the end, she put the house in London in Sami's name – supposedly so that she could go on claiming benefits – and despite not being at all happy with what she'd done, Hassan was careful not to say too much about it.

He didn't give up trying to persuade Mum to marry him, however, and he'd often cite the fact that he was still with her as 'proof' of his good intentions towards us all, saying, 'Look, I'm living here and helping you with the kids, aren't I? We're a family. Why not get married?' Sometimes, Mum would dare to say to him, 'Before I agree to marry you, I think you should see someone about your anger. You need to get it under control before you seriously hurt someone.' As if to prove that what she said was right, he'd then fly into a rage and start throwing things and smashing up the furniture, and Sami, Asha and I would run upstairs, praying that he wouldn't follow us. Occasionally, however, Hassan reacted more calmly: as we held our breath and waited for him to start shouting, he'd say instead, 'Yeah, you're right. Perhaps I will try to sort it out.' I don't know if he meant it when he said it, or if he wanted a British passport so badly that he managed to keep his temper and tell Mum what he knew she wanted to hear. But it didn't matter what he *said*; he still didn't do anything to try to curb his anger, and Mum still stayed with him, which meant that we did too.

Even after Mum and Dad were divorced and the meetings with Dad stopped and we lost contact with him, I don't think I completely gave up hope that my parents would get back together and that we'd live with him again. Mum told me many years later that if Dad had 'acted like a man' when he found out that Hassan was living with us, she'd probably have gone back to him. That just made me feel worse about everything that had happened, because it made it seem as if it was all just a game to her and it wouldn't really have mattered who she was married to. I don't think I could ever have explained to her or to anyone else how much it mattered to *me*, and to my brother and sister, too. In a way, I hope she did love Hassan, because otherwise it was all completely pointless and stupid and I was abused for all those years simply because she allowed herself to be flattered and cajoled into leaving Dad and then simply didn't have whatever it took – courage, energy, common sense – to get her and us out of what had turned out to be a very bad situation and go home.

Maybe Hassan loved Mum too, and maybe he didn't lure her away from Dad just to get a British passport. I do think that must be true, because surely it would have been much easier for him to marry a woman who wasn't already married and didn't have children. Or perhaps Mum's children were part of the attraction for him, because we provided him with easy targets for his bullying and abuse.

One morning, when I was twelve, Mum got dressed in her best Indian suit. When I asked her why, she clicked her tongue and said, 'No reason. It's nothing. I've just got to do something.' Whatever it was she was going to do, she didn't look very happy about it and I kept asking her, 'What, Mum? What have you got to do?' Eventually, as she was opening the front door to go out, she told me impatiently, 'I've just got to sign some papers.'

I didn't see her come back, but later that day she told me that she'd married Hassan.

'I thought you didn't want to marry him,' I said. 'Why didn't you say anything? Why did you just go off and do it without telling us?' I watched her face as I questioned her, and her expression echoed the resigned tone of her voice when she answered, 'Well, I suppose you could call it getting married. It's just to let him stay here.' Then she turned away from me and didn't talk about it again.

So Hassan got the British passport he'd wanted for so long, and Sami, Asha and I gained a stepfather.

Shortly afterwards, we left Manchester and returned to live in London. Mum had always complained about how cold it was in Manchester, and Hassan, who was struggling to find work, was convinced – rightly, as it turned out – that he would find a job easily in London. For me, moving away from Manchester meant leaving behind all the racial abuse and the feeling I'd always had there that I was an outcast.

In London, Hassan continued to sexually abuse me. I still hated what he did to me and it still made me feel that I didn't matter and didn't have any control over any aspect of my life, but by that time I'd accepted that I couldn't do anything about it and I'd learned to live with it. I hadn't thought that it could get any worse, and then Hassan had full sex with me for the first time.

I'd got home from school early one day and Mum left me alone with him while she went to pick up Asha. As soon as the front door had closed behind her, he told me to go up to their bedroom.

When he made me lie on the bed, I thought I knew what was coming. I did what I'd taught myself to do over the last couple of years, and imagined that my body wasn't really part of *me*. I'd just managed to detach my mind from what he was doing when I felt a pain like a red-hot poker being forced up inside me.

When I screamed, Hassan immediately pulled away from me, and I was sobbing as I said, 'Please, don't do that. It really hurt. I can't believe you did that.'

'You'll *have* to do it one day,' he told me. 'In fact, by the time you're sixteen, you'll be doing it *every* day.' He laughed in a sneering sort of way when he said it, but I noticed that he glanced several times towards the door, as if he was listening for the sound of Mum coming back. 'I'm sorry,' he said after a moment, when I was still sniffing miserably. 'It was a mistake, an accident. I didn't mean to do that. I just slipped. Put your clothes on and go downstairs, and make sure you pull yourself together before your mum gets back.'

I *did* try to do what he said, but when Mum came home I wasn't able to disguise the fact that I was upset, and eventually she asked me, irritably, 'Are you all right? You're very quiet. Has something happened?'

'I just don't feel very well,' I told her. Despite not wanting her to know Hassan's secret – because I thought it would make her sad – I had a fleeting hope that she'd ask me more questions and keep asking them until I told her the truth, because then it wouldn't be a secret any more and Hassan would have to stop. But she just shrugged and said, 'Did you get the dishes done?'

I felt hurt and angry. She was my mother, so surely she should have been able to tell that there was something wrong? I wouldn't have told her, because that would have negated everything I'd gone through for the past few years to try to protect her, but it would have been nice to feel she cared enough to want to know. Perhaps if she had asked questions and had shown any signs of being interested in me, Hassan might have been so afraid of being found out that he wouldn't have dared do it in the first place.

Instead, over the next few weeks, he did what he must always have intended to do, and I discovered that however bad things are, they can get worse. Thankfully, however, he didn't have very many opportunities to have full intercourse with me now that we were back in London: Mum didn't take Sami with her every time she went out, so I wasn't alone in the house with Hassan as often as I had been when we were in Manchester.

Hassan never used a condom, but sometimes he'd give me a small pill to take, either immediately afterwards or the next day, saying that it was 'just to make you feel better'. In fact, the pills made me incredibly sick and I'd sometimes vomit repeatedly for two or three days after I'd taken one. Even when I was so sick that I had to stay off school, however, I still don't remember Mum ever asking me any questions about what might have made me ill. Later, when I finally understood that they must have been morning-after pills, I worried in case they'd caused me lasting damage – making me sterile, for example.

Hassan would also often come into my bedroom at night: I'd wake up to find him standing in the darkness beside my bed. Sometimes, I'd still be half-awake when the door opened slowly, and I'd quickly shut my eyes and pray that he'd think I was asleep and wouldn't do anything to me. But I don't think it would have made any difference to Hassan if I was asleep or even dead. He'd stand in the doorway for a moment, listening to the sound of Asha's breathing, and when he was sure that she wasn't awake, he'd sit down on my bed and slide his thick, calloused fingers under my duvet.

One night, I'd pretended to be asleep when he came into the room and I lay perfectly still in my bed, breathing evenly, until I thought he'd gone out again. When I opened my eyes, he was standing in the beam of light that was cast across the bedroom floor from the lamp on the landing, looking at me with an expression that seemed to say clearly, 'I can wait. I'll be back.' Then he turned and walked silently out of the bedroom, and I lay awake for what felt like hours, dreading what he'd do to me when he returned.

Hassan had been talking for some time about the need to find me a husband. I wasn't even thirteen years old, so I couldn't believe he really meant it, or that Mum would consider it as a serious suggestion. I knew she'd been only thirteen when she came to England and married my father, but that was different: she'd lived all her life until then in India, where it was normal for girls to get married very young, often without ever having met their husbands before their wedding day, whereas I was English; I'd been brought up in England and I didn't *feel* Indian. So the thought of being forced into an arranged marriage – especially one arranged by Hassan – filled me with dread.

'Zara *should* be married,' Hassan often told Mum. 'She doesn't need to go to school. What good is an education to her? All she needs is a husband.' And, to my dismay, Mum didn't disagree.

After we'd left Manchester when I was twelve and returned to London, I settled down quite well and made some friends at my new school. Most of the pupils were Asian. Ironically, however, I didn't really fit in with them, and the friends I made were the other girls who didn't fit in either – the only two white girls in my class and a black girl.

I'd been incredibly anxious about having to start all over again at yet another school, and I'd been there for less than a week when the skin on my face erupted into red, angry-looking boils. I was devastated. When I showed them to Mum and asked her what I could do to make them better, she just shrugged and told me not to make such a fuss. So I went to school feeling sick with embarrassment and dread, and I hadn't even walked in through the school gates when a boy pointed at me and shouted that I had a face like a chocolate chip cookie. The boils lasted for about a month before gradually fading and disappearing, throughout which time people continued to make jokes about the way I looked. I tried to laugh it off, but it really hurt me.

The one good thing that came out of it all was that my new friend Sarah stood up for me whenever anyone teased me, which was a new experience for me and which seemed to prove that she really liked me. I was happy with my little group of friends and the fact that I wasn't alone any more. My form teacher was nice to me too, encouraging me and taking an interest in my progress at school. So I was appalled and very anxious about what Hassan was suggesting, and I begged Mum not to take any notice of him.

'I *like* school,' I told her. 'And I *do* need to go. Don't listen to him, Mum. You know what he's saying isn't right.'

'Well, I don't know,' Mum said. 'We'll see.' And my heart sank still further because I knew that if she made up her mind based on her own, often incomprehensible, form of logic, there would be nothing I could say that would influence the decision she'd made.

By the time I arrived at the school, my class had already started having sex education lessons and Hassan made Mum write a letter to say I wasn't allowed to go to them. So while the lessons were taking place, I had to sit on a step outside the classroom, feeling humiliated and, once again, different. I imagine Hassan told Mum that learning about sex wasn't appropriate for a young Muslim girl, but I think the real reason was that he was afraid that when I was taught about sex, I'd know what he was doing to me. And it worked, for a while at least, because I was much older than most girls are by the time I fully understood.

Even before I knew anything about sex, I'd started

trying to resist him again. I'd sometimes ask him, 'Why are you doing this? It isn't right. I'm your stepdaughter, so why don't you treat me like a daughter?' And he'd say, 'You're not like a daughter to me. You're special, and as soon as you're sixteen we're going to run away together and get married.'

I don't know if he really believed that that would ever happen – or even if he really would have wanted it to – but he said it with a conviction that made me feel sick and helpless. Despite telling myself that it would be all right because as soon as I was sixteen I knew that I'd be able to leave school, which meant that I could get a job, move out of the house and make my own decisions, it was difficult to imagine that the time would ever come when I would be allowed to make decisions about anything.

Sami had stopped going to school and was clearly very ill, and perhaps it was because his illness gave him some degree of protection against Hassan's violent attacks that my stepfather seemed to take every opportunity now to challenge and hurt me. I knew that what he was doing was sending me a message: don't try to confront me; just do as I say or your life won't be worth living. And Mum simply accepted his explanations for punishing me, apparently oblivious to – or choosing to ignore – the fact that he'd often react to something trivial I'd done wrong by hitting me so hard that he sent me sprawling across the floor. She accepted it, too, when Hassan refused to let me do anything or go anywhere outside of school where I might come into contact with boys. So when the school organised a trip that would involve being away for a couple of days, Mum just shrugged and said 'Okay' when Hassan told her, 'The only reason girls want to go on these trips is to get together with boys.' It might have made me laugh if I hadn't been so disappointed, because it seemed to me that the only place where I was at risk in any way was my own home.

What made it all even more unfair, however, was the fact that he allowed my sister to do a lot of the 'normal' things I wanted to do, such as wear Western clothes and go out to play with her friends. Apparently, whereas he didn't really mind what Asha did, he was determined to keep me firmly under his control. When I railed against the injustice of it all, he said, 'It's because you've got a different sort of figure. You've always been more developed than your sister, so you need to keep your body covered up and stay at home.'

He'd often tell me that, 'In our faith, girls and young women don't have *friendships* with boys.' I knew better than to remind him that it was *his* faith, not strictly mine, and that as I'd been born and raised in England and considered myself to be English, it seemed only reasonable that I wanted to live my life like any other English teenager would do. I didn't ask him, either, what he thought boys might do to hurt or shame me that he hadn't done to me already.

Perhaps the restrictions he imposed on me and the concerns he voiced repeatedly about all the evil predators who were waiting for the opportunity to put an end to the innocence of any good Muslim girl they encountered were simply his way of making sure that I knew he was in charge and that I remained under his control.

After Hassan had married Mum and finally got his British passport, he was able to travel out of the country for the first time since he'd entered it illegally several years previously, and not long after we'd gone to live in London, we went, as a family, to visit his relatives in Morocco for eight weeks.

Hassan was violent, bad tempered and abusive, Sami was withdrawn and often behaved very strangely, and Mum and Hassan had never previously taken us anywhere, so the prospect of us all going on a 'holiday' together was unnerving. But, as we'd be staying in other people's houses, at least I knew that it would be very difficult for Hassan to do anything to me while we were away.

When we arrived in Morocco, we stayed with one of Hassan's brothers, who was married and had four boisterous children. Morocco seemed more alien to me than India had done. In India I'd felt welcome and, despite not speaking the language very well, I could understand what people were saying. There were things I liked about Morocco, but there were some aspects of the culture and the life there that I didn't understand, such as the attitude many people seemed to have towards animals.

Although I've always loved animals, I realise there's a huge difference between the way I feel about my pets and the way someone feels about the animals they're raising on a farm, particularly a very poor farm like some of those we saw in Morocco. Even so, I was upset by the cruelty shown by Hassan's nieces and nephews to the cats that lived -- apparently unfed and uncared for -- on the balconies of their house. The children would often pick the kittens up by their tails, spin them round their heads a few times and then throw them across to another balcony, while Hassan and his brother and sister-in-law watched and laughed.

I've never been able to understand how you can

expect anyone to show compassion for other human beings if they haven't been taught from an early age to respect *all* living creatures, and to do them no harm. I felt that by spending time with his family, I was gaining an insight into why Hassan had such a harsh outlook on life. But I'd suffered too much for too long at his hands for what I was learning to make me feel sympathetic towards him in any way.

After we'd stayed in the town for a few days, Hassan's brother drove us in his truck into the countryside, along steep, unmade roads with spectacular views, into the hills, where the brilliance of the sun seemed to bring everything into clear, sharp focus.

When we arrived at Hassan's parents' farm, we were met by his father, who was like an older, thinner version of his son except for the fact that his face was so wizened it looked as if it was made out of dense, scrunched-up leather. He was standing outside a low, rectangular building that at first sight appeared to have been cut from a solid lump of stone. When Hassan jumped out of the truck and ran towards him, there were tears in his eyes and an expression of unequivocal affection on his face that I'd never seen before.

Inside, the house was like a cave with sheepskins and tapestries on almost every wall. We sat on rugs on the floor to drink the pungent green tea his father made for us and to eat the meal prepared by his mother, whose face was almost as wrinkled and weather-beaten as her husband's.

The thin, sparse soil on the land around the house was so littered with stones it was barely visible, but somehow it had given rise to a mass of orange trees, and the sheep grazing on it had bells around their necks that filled the air with sound. The place where Hassan had grown up was beautiful, but it soon became clear that making a living there was tough, hard work, and I could see why he might have wanted to make a 'better' life for himself elsewhere.

The day after we arrived at the farm, Hassan's father killed a sheep to welcome his son home, and perhaps to welcome his new daughter-in-law and her children, too. I wasn't sure how my step-grandparents felt about us, particularly as they barely spoke to us – or, in fact, to Hassan.

Hassan's father slit the sheep's throat right outside the open door of the room where we were sitting. At first, the poor creature lay motionless on the dusty ground; then its body suddenly began to convulse and blood started to spurt out of the wound on its neck. Hassan's mother was watching us – as she almost always was –

and although I was anxious not to offend his family, I burst into tears. The old woman just shrugged, and I heard Hassan's father say something to his son in a sharp tone before turning away and beginning to strip the skin off the carcass with a knife.

That night, Hassan's mother made a stew that smelt of ginger and cinnamon, but neither my desire to be polite nor my fear of Hassan could induce me to eat it.

It was on that same day that we met Hassan's younger brother, Khalid, for the first time. Khalid was almost the spitting image of Hassan, except that he was clean-shaven and less rough-looking. As the youngest of the five brothers, Khalid was the only one who remained unmarried and hadn't moved away from the farm to live in a town. Despite the fact that he didn't speak English and we didn't speak Arabic, it was clear that he wanted to be friendly. But, as I was thirteen and he was thirty – not much younger than my mother and Hassan – I had no interest in him.

Later that evening, I heard Hassan say to Mum, 'If she married Khalid, she could stay here in Morocco, and that would be a good thing, because in England she's going to start going with boys. I've noticed already that she has an eye for the men.' He'd said something similar to Mum in front of me a couple of days previously, when he'd told her, 'If Zara doesn't leave England, she's going to be corrupted and ruined.' It had seemed ridiculous at the time, particularly because it wasn't true that I had 'an eye for the men' – I'd never shown any interest in boys at all – and because Hassan himself had been 'corrupting' me since I was seven years old. So when I heard them talking that night and realised that it was Hassan's intention to marry me off to his brother, I felt panic-stricken.

The next morning, when Mum asked me what I thought about Khalid, I told her urgently, 'I won't be ruined, Mum. I promise I won't. Don't make me stay here, please. I'm too young to get married. Please, Mum. You *can't* take me out of school. People *do* need to be educated. Girls need to go to school just as much as boys do.'

'Well, maybe that's true,' she said. 'But he thinks it's a good idea, so maybe he's right.'

'You don't have to do *everything* he says,' I told her, trying to sound reasonable rather than as desperate as I felt. 'I mean, it's sick if you really think about it. He's my stepdad and he's trying to get me married off to his brother, who's almost the same age as *he* is. That's wrong. Surely you can see that?'

'Hmm, well, I suppose it's possible that his brother

just wants a passport,' Mum answered. I stared at her in amazement: what other reason did she think Hassan could have had other than to secure a British passport for his brother? Then she shrugged her shoulders and I could see she'd lost interest in the conversation. All I could do was try to refresh her doubts whenever the opportunity arose.

Although there were lots of reasons not to enjoy being in Morocco, at least I didn't have to worry very much for a whole eight weeks about what Hassan might do to me. He did abuse me while we were there, but not very often, because he didn't often get the chance. Then, one day, when he'd found some excuse to take me up to the top floor of his brother's house, he put his hand inside my pants and touched me. I cried out in pain. It felt as if my skin was on fire, and nothing I did afterwards to try to make it better did anything to lessen the almost unbearable itching and stinging.

At home when Hassan had sex with me, it always made me feel dirty and disgusting, and I'd scrub my body and wash my private parts over and over again, trying to get rid of his smell and make myself clean. I didn't know why I was always sore; I think I just assumed it was 'normal'. But on another day when we were in Morocco and Hassan tried to have sex with me at his brother's house, it was more painful than it had ever been before and I cried so much that he had to satisfy himself.

Later, when I washed myself yet again with soap and hot water, it seemed that however hard I scrubbed, I couldn't get clean and over the next few days, the pain grew steadily worse. I didn't know what to do about it. Because I thought it was related to what Hassan did to me, I knew I couldn't ask Mum. So I kept on scrubbing myself with soap and hot water, without realising that what I was doing was simply exacerbating the rash.

Eventually, whatever was wrong with me cured itself and despite the fact that the pain and itching almost drove me mad, there was an upside, because Hassan left me alone for as long as the infection lasted.

When we were back in England, Hassan continued to try to get Mum to agree to my marrying his brother. Then one day I heard her tell him, 'I think Khalid is too old for Zara.' I could feel tears of relief pricking my eyes until she added, 'Although I do think you might be right about taking her out of school.' My heart began to thud and a sour, acidic taste burned the back of my throat so that I couldn't swallow. I knew Hassan would have realised, as I did, that Mum hadn't really made a decision about it, and that if he persisted, he still might be able to persuade her to agree to my leaving school and marrying his brother. I knew, too, that without school there'd be *nothing* positive in my life at all, and that I'd have nowhere to go where I felt normal and safe, and nowhere to escape from Hassan.

I really liked my teachers, and I did sometimes think about telling one of them what he was doing to me. I felt instinctively that they'd listen and take me seriously. What always stopped me was my fear of what the consequences might be. I know that some people are impatient with the concept that anyone other than a very young child ever has to 'put up with' sexual abuse, and to some extent I can understand why they might think like that. I'm sure it's hard for anyone who hasn't suffered long-term abuse to understand the effect it has and how it completely destroys your confidence and makes you believe that you have no influence or control over anything, including – and most importantly – any aspect of your own life.

Children who've been abused grow up feeling guilty about everything. They learn to be afraid – afraid of the person who's abusing them; of what that person is going to do to them; of what would happen to them if they told anyone the secret their abuser has always insisted they must keep; and of what other people would think about them if anyone ever found out … the list of fears is endless.

I wanted to tell my teachers because I thought they might be able to make it stop. But it never seriously crossed my mind that I had the power to do anything to help myself. Every time I was on the brink of saying something, an image would flash into my mind of Mum sitting on the sofa with her hands folded in her lap, sobbing, while my brother was led away by the police, because they believed Hassan's story that Sami was the one who'd been abusing me and that I was lying to try to protect him. It was what Hassan had told me countless times would happen if I revealed 'our secret'.

'Sami's behaviour is so strange that no one would doubt my word if I told them that he's been having sex with you,' Hassan told me. And I was convinced that he was right.

Despite not being able to tell my teachers, however, school was the one place I felt encouraged and comfortable in my own skin. I always found comfort in the thought that my teachers liked me and cared about me, and I know that without their encouragement I'd have had no positive influence in my life at all.

One day, after we'd got back from Morocco, someone came to my school to give a talk about bullying. While they were there, they put posters up on the walls, and on some of the posters there was a phone number for the Samaritans. The woman who gave the talk said that anyone could call the number and that, without having to give their name, they would be able to talk to someone who'd understand how they felt about being bullied. Over the next few days, I came close to phoning the number, not because I thought that I was a victim of bullying – although, in a sense, I was – but because what the woman said about how bullying makes people feel sounded a lot like the way I felt about what Hassan was doing to me.

In the end, I didn't pick up the telephone because I was afraid of what the consequences might be – for me, Mum, Sami and Asha – if I said anything, and because the worst fear of all is the fear of the unknown. Children – even children in their teens – can't really imagine things they haven't ever experienced, and I really did believe that Sami might be locked away in a prison. So I told myself that I was doing something good by keeping quiet and saving other people from being hurt and, eventually, I threw away the phone number I'd scribbled on to a piece paper.

I didn't know what the future held in store for me, but I was increasingly certain that whatever it was, it wasn't going to be any better than the last six years had been. And that's when I began to realise that I *had* to find some way of loosening Hassan's grip on Mum, and on all of us, before it was too late.

Chapter Nine

THE FIRST HOUSE we lived in when we moved back to London had a big garden and, one day, Hassan told me to meet him in the shed.

'I can't,' I said. 'I've got to do my homework and I ...'

He cut me off, narrowing his eyes the way he did when he was silently daring you to argue with him, saying, 'Ten minutes.'

Ten minutes later, I stood with my fingers touching the handle on the back door of the house, thinking, *If I stand here and count to ten, something will happen so that I won't have to go.* I counted to ten again after the first time, and then I opened the door, stepped out into the warmth of the early evening sunshine that still flooded the garden, and walked slowly across the grass.

'Look at this.' Hassan held out a magazine towards me as soon as I opened the door of the shed, and I glanced down at the open page. At first I couldn't make any sense of what he was showing me. Then I took an involuntary step backwards, away from Hassan and the horrible photograph, and said, 'I don't *want* to look at it. That's disgusting.'

'But you *need* to see it,' he laughed, reaching out his hand and locking his strong fingers around my wrist. 'This is what women do.'

The woman in the picture was kneeling on the floor in front of a man whose penis seemed to be in her mouth. I didn't know *what* she was doing but, whatever it was, I knew with absolute certainty that *I* was never going to do it to anyone.

Hassan released his grip on my arm and I took another step away from him. When I glanced up again, he'd pulled down his trousers and underpants.

'Just do what the woman in the photograph's doing,' he told me, and I retched as I fumbled behind my back for the catch that held the wooden door of the shed closed.

'No! I'm not going to do that. Just leave me alone,' I almost shouted at him.

I scraped the tips of my fingers across the rough, splintered wood of the door when I pushed it open, barely noticing that they hurt as I fled, sobbing, through the last patch of sunlight that remained in the garden, and into the house.

'What's the matter with you?' Mum asked crossly as I came hurtling through the back door just as she walked into the kitchen. 'What have you been doing? Where is *he*?'

It was odd the way my mother almost never used Hassan's name. Even years later, she'd sometimes say something about 'him' and when I asked her who she meant, it was only her refusal to say his name that gave me the answer to my question.

'He's in the shed,' I told her now. Then I ran out of the kitchen and up the stairs to my bedroom, where I sat on my bed with my hands clasped tightly around my knees, trying to blot out the horrible picture that was in my mind.

Later that evening, when Mum called us for supper, Hassan was crossing the hallway from the living room as I walked down the stairs.

'You're not being very nice to me,' he said, glancing quickly over his shoulder and speaking in a quiet, low voice. 'And you know I don't like it when you're not nice to me. It's foolish of you anyway, because you'll have to do what I want you to do in the end. So, really, it's better for *everyone* if you don't make me angry.'

'I'm not going to do *that*,' I hissed at him, frightened by his threat but still so repulsed by the photograph he'd shown me that I knew I could never bring myself to do it, whatever punishment he thought up for me. 'You're my stepfather – you're almost my father – so why can't you treat me like a daughter?'

Hassan smiled and said softly, 'I'm going to make you pay for it.' Then he turned his back on me and walked into the kitchen.

He didn't speak to me at all during supper that evening. Afterwards, when I was sitting watching television with Sami, Asha and Mum, and had just begun to wonder if he'd decided to let it drop after all, we heard him shout and then call Mum's name. Mum stood up wearily and walked to the foot of the stairs. Hassan was standing in the open doorway of Sami's bedroom.

'Look! Look at this!' He bellowed. 'Look what that little shit's got hidden under his bed.'

My heart had started to race when I'd first heard Hassan shout and I'd followed Mum out of the living room into the hallway. Hassan held out his hands to show her what looked like a small pile of magazines.

'There's a whole box of them,' he raged. 'That's it! That's enough! Where are you, you sick little bastard?'

As Hassan pounded down the stairs, I turned to look through the open living-room door at Sami. He was still sitting on the sofa, his lower jaw rigid as if he was clenching his teeth, a glazed look of fear in his eyes that made me think of a cornered animal that's so frightened it doesn't know which way to turn to try to escape.

Hassan walked into the living room and then seemed almost to fly across it with all the destructive force of a tornado. Before Sami had even had a chance to react, Hassan had thrown a magazine into his face, dragged him on to the floor with one hand and was punching him repeatedly in the head with the other. Asha was sobbing and Mum was pulling at Hassan's arms and saying, 'No, no. Get off him. You're going to hurt him. Stop! Stop!'

Eventually, Hassan did stop kicking and hitting poor Sami, but he still kept one hand clasped firmly around my brother's skinny arm as he pulled him up off the floor and on to his feet. I could see that Mum was shaking as she asked Hassan, 'Why are you so angry with him? What has he done?'

'I'll show you what he's done,' Hassan shouted. 'Go upstairs and have a look.' He turned and spat the words into Sami's face as he said them, and I saw Sami flinch and turn his head away.

Asha and I followed Mum upstairs. When she bent down and picked up a cardboard box from the floor beside Sami's bed, I heard her gasp.

'What? What is it, Mum?' I asked her.

For a few seconds she didn't answer, and then she said, 'He's right. Sami shouldn't be reading things like this.' She dropped the magazine back into the box and then half turned away from us as she put it on the floor. But I didn't have to see it to know what was in it.

'They're *not* Sami's,' I said quietly.

'What do you mean? What do you know about it?' She sounded distressed and upset as well as angry. 'Of course they're Sami's. Who else would they belong to? They were under his bed.'

'I can't explain how I know,' I told her. 'Honestly, Mum, they're not his.'

She pushed me out of the way impatiently and I followed her back down the stairs. Sami was sitting silently on the sofa, the handful of magazines Hassan had brought downstairs with him lying, unopened, on his lap where Hassan had thrown them.

'They're not mine, Mum, I promise,' Sami whispered. 'I've never seen them before.'

However, the evidence appeared to speak for itself and it was clear that Mum didn't believe him.

The next day, when I asked Hassan if the magazines were the same ones he'd shown me in the shed, he smiled a smugly spiteful half-smile and said,

'Anything's possible. Perhaps next time you'll do what I tell you to do.' I could feel my eyes filling with tears. No wonder Sami always seemed so bemused and lost, as if he didn't understand what was going on in the world around him.

When Hassan first came to live with us in Manchester, Sami had been really excited about having his 'good friend' there. But as the weeks passed and he kept trying and failing to make Hassan like him, I'd sometimes felt like crying when I saw the bewildered hurt in his eyes. For years, Hassan had been bullying him and beating him for no real reason at all. So it was little wonder that Sami had simply given up trying to make sense of *anything*.

What seemed so unfair on that occasion was that my brother was so innocent he probably didn't even know magazines like that existed, and he certainly wouldn't have dared to buy one if he did. His behaviour was often odd and he didn't ever really talk to any of us any more – at least, not in a way that made any sense. But he was my brother and I loved him, and so the next time Hassan showed me a picture in one of his magazines, I did the vile, horrible thing he wanted me to do, and then I vomited into the towel he pushed into my hands when I started to retch.

A few days later, when he made me go to the shed with him again, he told me that he wanted me to swallow the repulsive, foul-smelling stuff that came out of his penis. At first I refused and then I thought about what he'd done to Sami and I tried to do it. But I began to choke and had to spit it out into a towel. Hassan was angry with me and told me to get out of the shed. That evening, when we were watching television, he found some excuse to shout at me and then he punched the side of my head.

Over the next few days, he continued to try to cajole and coerce me into doing what he wanted me to do. 'You *need* to do this,' he'd tell me angrily. 'I don't know why you're resisting it. It only takes a second.' I couldn't understand why it was so important to him; but it didn't matter how angry he was with me, it made me choke and I simply couldn't do it.

Then one day he told me, 'I went to the doctor yesterday and had an injection so that I can do something to help *you*.' He sounded almost fatherly and I was immediately wary. 'I know you've always wanted to look more like your mother,' he said, smiling at me sympathetically. 'And, because of this special injection I've had, if you do what I'm asking you to do, your eyes will become lighter so that you'll look just like her.' And, as ridiculous as it sounds now, I believed him.

It wasn't so much that I wanted to look like my mother; it was just that because she never seemed to tire of telling me that my skin and my eyes were too dark, I thought that if they were like hers, she might love me. So I tried really hard to swallow the revolting stuff that came out of Hassan and, sometimes, I did manage to do what he so insistently wanted me to do.

A few days later, I was looking in the mirror in the hallway when Mum came out of the kitchen and asked what I was doing.

'I'm going to be beautiful soon,' I told her, with more conviction than I really felt. 'My eyes are going to get lighter, like yours.'

Mum laughed. 'Oh, really?' she said. 'And what's going to make your eyes change colour?'

I just smiled and told her, 'It's a secret. You'll see.'

And although it hadn't happened immediately, as I'd hoped it would, so that I wouldn't have to keep doing the disgusting thing Hassan made me do, I still believed that it *would* happen. I looked in the mirror every single day for the next few weeks, and sometimes almost managed to convince myself that the colour of my eyes *had* lightened. I think I knew in my heart that they hadn't, but it still didn't even cross my mind that Hassan had lied to me, not least because, for as long as I could remember, I'd believed the things he told me.

Since the age of seven, I'd lived in dread of hearing the sound of the front door closing when Mum went out with Sami and Asha, because I knew that Hassan would wait for maybe a minute or two and then tell me to go upstairs. And then I'd have to lie on the bed while he touched me and made me touch him or while he had full sex with me, depending on how long he thought Mum would be gone.

Hassan still talked about the time when we would 'run away' together, when I was sixteen. I couldn't understand why he believed that I actually *wanted* to be with him. He must have known I hated doing the things he made me do, otherwise I don't know how he explained to himself the fact that he often had to threaten to hurt me or my brother to make me do them. He talked about 'our future' as if it was a reward he was going to give me; whereas, in reality, just the thought of it made me feel so panic-stricken I could hardly breathe.

My only comfort was thinking that I still had time to plan how I was going to escape from him or that some-thing would happen that would change the way things were. But it was difficult to believe that I'd ever get away, because Hassan had controlled every part of my life for so long, I couldn't imagine what it would be like not to be watching and waiting all the time to see what he was going to do next.

After Mum and Hassan were married and Hassan had a British passport, he got a job at a big hotel near where we were living. He'd sometimes think up an excuse to take me there with him. The first time, we went to the kitchens, which were on the ground floor at the back of the main building, and he introduced me to some of his work colleagues. They were nice people – and very nice to me – but I felt uncomfortable because, despite not knowing why Hassan had taken me there, I did know that there was a reason for it: he never did anything without a reason.

We sat in a little staffroom next to the main kitchen with some of his co-workers while Hassan drank a cup of coffee. Then he pushed his chair away from the table and, as he stood up, he said casually, 'I've just come in to have a quick look at a broken sash cord in a window in one of the bedrooms.' He laughed and reached out a hand to squeeze my upper arm as he added, 'You should feel her muscles! This girl's as strong as any boy her age. That's why she's such a help with DIY jobs.'

I blushed with embarrassment. Everyone else simply accepted his explanation of why I was there with him. But I knew that it was an excuse for whatever it was he really intended to do. As I followed him out of the kitchen and down a dimly lit passageway, the palms of my hands were sweating and I felt sick.

We walked up the stairs to the first floor, where Hassan paused outside the door of one of the bedrooms. He asked, as if he was offering me a treat, 'Shall we go in here?'

I wanted to shout at him, 'No! Don't you under-stand? I don't *want* to do the things you make me do. I hate you, and I hate the disgusting things you do to me. So don't try to make yourself feel better about it by pretending that I'm doing it willingly.' But I was still too afraid of him to say anything other than, 'I don't think we should. We've been away so long Mum will be starting to wonder where we are.' And, to my relief, he seemed to agree.

On other days when he took me with him to the hotel, he'd say, 'I could get a room and we could do it here? Would you like that?' And I'd feel the panic rising up inside me as I told him, 'Not today; maybe we could do it another day.'

I suppose the fact that I was trying to placate him so

that he wouldn't be angry did nothing to dispel what he'd already decided to believe about my willingness to have sex with him. I was conditioned never to oppose him directly – something he'd reminded me of unequivocally when he attacked Sami after he 'found' the magazines in his bedroom – and I believed that saying 'No' to him about anything simply wasn't an option. Although I knew I'd have to do it eventually, I kept hoping that if I could stall him for long enough, something might happen so that I wouldn't.

Hassan was cautious because he was afraid of getting caught, but the day did come when he took me into one of the hotel bedrooms, locked the door and had sex with me. On that occasion, I didn't manage to close my mind to what he was doing to me, as I'd taught myself to do over the years, because I was so intent on listening for the sound of footsteps approaching along the corridor. I'd begun to understand that what Hassan was doing was having sex with me. I knew I couldn't do anything to stop him, but I felt guilty about it nonetheless, as if it was somehow my fault. So just the thought of a hotel guest or a member of staff opening the door of the bedroom and finding us there made me feel sick with shame and humiliation.

Sometimes, Hassan would tell Mum that he had to

go out to buy something at the local DIY shop. I'd be holding my breath and praying that he'd just go, when he'd add, casually, as if it was an afterthought, 'I might as well take Zara with me.' I could never understand why Mum didn't ask *why* he wanted to take me with him to buy a screwdriver, or why he didn't suggest taking Sami or Asha instead. But she didn't; she'd barely look up from what she was doing as I followed Hassan out to the car.

He'd usually only drive a short distance from the house before stopping at the side of the road and pushing his hand roughly inside my pants, touching me in the way that always made my skin crawl. Afterwards, even when I'd washed and scrubbed my body, I still sometimes imagined I could smell him. Often when he was abusing me, he'd try to kiss me and my mouth would be full of the acrid taste of his foul-smelling breath as he forced his tongue down my throat until I gagged and retched. I hated it even more than I hated him touching me with his fingers. The repulsive taste of cigarettes stayed in my mouth for hours afterwards and I'd imagine that his saliva was still there, too. However hard I scrubbed my lips with a scouring pad so that they bled and my mouth became encircled by sores that looked like blisters, I still felt dirty.

The belief that I was dirty had been with me since my early childhood when my mother used to call me the Urdu word, *mela* – filthy. When we moved to Manchester and I went to school every day without washing and wearing stained clothes, I'd thought that Mum was right. And then Hassan called me dirty too, because of what he was doing to me. So I suppose it's hardly surprising that it was an anxiety that never left me. In fact, I still shower twice every day, but at least I now realise that that has more to do with psychology than cleanliness.

The only time I could ever be sure of having a break from Hassan's abuse was for the few days every month when I had my period, because he wouldn't touch me while I was 'unclean'. So it wasn't many months after my periods started that I began to pretend they lasted longer than they actually did. A few times I even got away with it for eight days, until Hassan became suspicious and said, 'They don't last that long,' and I had to tell him quickly that it was almost finished and I'd just wanted to be sure.

I suppose anyone can get used to anything if they have to and, although having to live with Hassan's abuse made me miserable and unable ever to relax, it was my life, and I didn't have any alternative other than to learn to accept it. At least in London I had lots of friends again and I was going to a school I liked, where the teachers encouraged me.

Otherwise, very little had changed. Sami was ill and strange and lived in a world of his own. Asha was old enough to try to avoid doing anything that might antagonise our stepfather – which unfortunately also meant that she was old enough to be included in his beatings whenever he lost his temper. Mum was sad and detached, as she'd always been. And Hassan still often erupted without cause or warning into apparently uncontrollable anger.

Financially, things were getting better for us now that Hassan was able to work at the hotel and Mum was doing sewing again. After a while, Mum sold the house she'd got in her divorce from Dad and bought another, larger one a few miles away for us all to live in.

Mum and Hassan had lots of arguments at that time, most of them because Hassan kept insisting that Mum should put the new house in both their names, and Mum kept refusing. She still said she had to make sure that the money was kept intact for her children, but I think Hassan knew that that was just an excuse. When she stood her ground however much he shouted at her, his frustration was almost palpable.

Before we could move into the new house, there was a lot of work that needed to be done to it, and Hassan often took me there with him at weekends and occasionally in the evenings after school to help. I liked doing the jobs he set me to do – I didn't even mind scrubbing every inch of the filthy kitchen – and what I particularly enjoyed was creating order out of the chaos in the garden. Any pleasure I might have had from doing the work, however, was far outweighed by the dread that seemed to expand inside me as I waited to hear Hassan's voice calling me from upstairs. In fact, I preferred the days when he took me into the bedroom as soon as we arrived at the house, because at least then, once it was over, I didn't have to spend the rest of the day with my stomach twisting itself into knots, wondering when it was going to happen.

I felt very vulnerable being alone with him on those visits to the empty house, knowing that he could spend as much time doing things to me as he wanted, safe in the knowledge that no one was going to interrupt him. Every time we went there I'd tell myself, 'Maybe today something will happen so that we'll have to go home early, and then he won't do it.' But he almost always did. He'd take me upstairs, to the one room that had a bed in it, and do things to me – some of which he'd never done before. Because he knew there was no risk of anyone hearing us or walking in on us, he didn't have to rush or do things only once; sometimes they seemed to go on forever.

He was trying to have anal sex with me. I didn't know that that was what he was doing when he made me lie on my stomach on the bed and pushed his finger into my bottom. It really hurt, but it wasn't until he began to rub his penis on me and then tried to force it inside me that I'd start to sob. So he pulled it out again, turned me over and had 'normal' sex with me instead.

My body has always been quite curvy and by the age of twelve I had well-developed breasts – a fact that was completely ignored by Mum, who didn't ever tell me that I should wear a bra, let alone take me out and buy one for me. One of the things Hassan started doing that he'd never done before was rubbing his penis between my breasts. I hated it, as I hated everything he did to me, but what I learned to dread even more was him coming all over my face, covering it in horrible, slimy mess that stung my eyes and smelt so disgusting that it made me retch.

It wasn't just the abusive things he was doing to me that made my misery feel like something real and solid that was pressing down on me like a weight; I felt helpless, like a young child again: no one was going to come to the house, no one would hear me if I cried out, and Hassan could do exactly what he wanted to do for as long as he wanted to do it. It was like being constantly reminded, every time he took me to the house, that I was trapped and that I had no control over anything.

When the work was finally done and we moved into the new house, I was given the only bedroom on the top floor. It was supposed to be a good thing because it meant that I no longer had to share a room with Asha, but it wasn't, because what it also meant was that at night I was cut off from everyone else and completely vulnerable to Hassan. Mum didn't seem to be suspicious whatever Hassan did, and because he'd long ago realised that she was rarely, if ever, going to ask any questions, he'd sometimes take me upstairs to my bedroom during the day, even when she was in the kitchen two floors below. So, after we moved, there was never any time of the day or night when I was safe from his abuse.

Perhaps it was as a result of getting away with *that* that Hassan had the confidence to touch me one evening when we were all together in the living room, watching television.

I was lying on the sofa under a blanket when he came into the room and sat down next to me. As he squeezed into the space between me and Sami, I was instantly alert. Then he lifted my legs and laid them across his knees, as if he was simply making more room for himself. I didn't really think he'd do anything in full view of everyone else. So when he slid his hands under the blanket, pushed them down inside my pants and forced his finger inside me, I couldn't believe that it was really happening.

For years he'd impressed upon me the importance of keeping 'our secret', although his reminders hadn't been necessary as soon as I was old enough to develop a sense of shame. And I could feel that shame now, burning my cheeks as I lay on the sofa, not daring to move and wishing that Hassan would stop. What he was doing didn't make any sense to me: I knew that the only thing he was really afraid of was being found out. Perhaps he just wanted to remind me that he was in control, because he didn't do it again after that day.

What it made me realise, however, was that Mum had absolutely no suspicion about what Hassan was doing to me, or she'd decided, for whatever reason, that she didn't *want* to know. The problem was that she rarely showed her emotions, so you could never guess what she was thinking. She didn't wail and screech when she was upset; she'd just sit down and sob quietly for a few minutes, and then she'd wipe her eyes and carry on with whatever she'd been doing. When Hassan was in a rage and beating one of us, she'd tug at his arm and say, 'Hey, hey. Get off. Leave it now. You'll hurt them.' But she didn't ever sound really angry with him.

I think I always believed that Mum wouldn't leave Hassan whatever he did, and that she loved him more than she loved Sami, Asha and me. She certainly never threatened to leave him when he hurt us, even on the occasion when Sami ended up in hospital and was so ill. And I believed, too, that she'd be very upset if she knew Hassan was sexually abusing me. So I had to keep Hassan's secret and, despite often feeling that I was carrying a burden that was far too heavy for me to carry on my own, I was proud of myself for protecting my mother and, as much as I was able to do so, my brother too.

Chapter Ten

THE RATIONAL PART of my brain tells me that what happened to me when I was a child wasn't in any way my fault. But I still feel guilty. I think people who've been abused feel that other people must think they could somehow have prevented it from happening to them, particularly when it continued beyond early childhood. And perhaps they almost believe that themselves, although the truth is that no one would *ever* 'allow' themselves to be abused if they thought there was any chance they could stop it happening.

Even when I was fourteen years old, I was too afraid to tell anyone about what Hassan was doing to me, or even to tell Hassan himself to stop. I know now, of course, that that's what I should have done. But at the time I didn't know that there was any other way, because I'd been conditioned and brainwashed, by fear and by threats that became realities, since I was seven years old into doing what Hassan told me to do.

Without being aware of it, we learn all sorts of things when we're young that we never even think to question. We're taught facts at school by our teachers, and others we learn – either directly or indirectly – at home from our parents, and it would be a very unusual child who doubted or disbelieved any of these 'facts'. Gradually, as we grow up, all our learned information builds into an understanding of the world and how it works. Children believe what they're told by the adults who control their lives, and they accept the normality that's presented to them. They don't question it; that's just the way it is.

As I got older, into my teens, and I began to hear my friends talking about sex, it did finally dawn on me what Hassan was doing to me, and that it was *wrong*. And that's when I started trying again to resist him. He responded by complaining about me to my mother, making up excuses so that he could punish me, such as, 'That daughter of yours is evil. All I asked her to do was take a dirty plate into the kitchen and she swore at me.' And my mother would look shocked and ask me if it was true.

'No, of course I didn't say that,' I'd tell her. 'You know I don't speak like that to anyone. Why would you believe *him* rather than me?'

Mum *did* seem to believe him, however, and she always took his side. She would often smack my face and say angrily, 'You're lying. You shouldn't speak to him like that.'

I knew she'd never see what was really happening right under her nose. I kept telling her – as I'd always done – that she shouldn't allow Hassan to hit us the way he did, and she kept doing what she'd always done and closed her mind to the facts.

Hassan constantly complained to Mum about Sami's behaviour too, and when Mum tried to defend Sami by saying, 'He's not well; he can't help it,' Hassan would sneer and tell her, 'I reckon he's putting it on. If he's still got a *jinn,* perhaps I should try again to beat it out of him.'

As Hassan's frustration grew, I began to dread getting home from school every day even more than I'd done for as long as I could remember. As soon as I opened the front door, I felt as if I was stepping into the world Hassan had created for us – a world of shouting and anger in which I could never relax, even for a moment.

I think that when I started to stand up to Hassan – very tentatively at first – and told him, 'What you're doing to me isn't right,' he realised that I was growing more confident and he must have wondered if he was losing his power over me and that, one day, I might actually tell someone. Eventually, perhaps because he was becoming less certain that he was in control of *me*, he started to take his anger out on Mum. Despite the fact that I hated them shouting at each other, when they began to row constantly I saw it as my chance to try to influence Mum so that she'd see him for what he really was. I'd take every opportunity to tell her, 'You can't put up with this. You've got to do something. He isn't a good person. You've got to leave him. It *is* possible, you know.' And despite never saying anything except 'Hmm', the fact that she wasn't angry with me made me wonder if she might actually be listening to what I was saying.

In the end, it was what Hassan himself did that changed everything – as had always been the case for as long as I could remember. This time, however, what he did was lose his temper, lash out and hit Mum.

After he'd done the same thing a few more times, she told him to leave.

I've always wanted to believe that there was another reason why she finally snapped and kicked Hassan out. For eight years, she'd allowed him to abuse her children – both physically and mentally – so I didn't want to accept that the one thing that made her draw the line was Hassan hitting *her*. On the day when everything changed, Asha and I were cowering in the living room out of the way while Mum and Hassan had a huge row in the kitchen. We could only hear snatches of what they were saying, and then Mum walked out of the kitchen into the hallway and Hassan followed her, shouting, 'If you don't do what I tell you, I'll get one of those fish hooks and hang your kids up on the door by their chins.'

The door of the living room was half open, and I could see the shocked expression on Mum's face. Hassan must have seen it too, because he suddenly grabbed her by the shoulders and started punching her on the side of the head. Fortunately, he stopped when I ran out into the hallway and tried to push myself between them, but not before he'd landed his last punch squarely on my jaw.

Mum told me later that she'd already begun to wonder before that day if Hassan was completely sane, and that that was the moment when she realised he was probably capable of murdering us all.

I think he hit her on a few more occasions after that and then, one night, I woke up to hear them bellowing at each other; it sounded as if they were in the kitchen. As I lay in bed listening, I thought I could hear something different in the tones of their voices that made me more than usually anxious. A loud thudding noise that was actually the beating of my heart seemed to be coming from somewhere inside my head, just behind my ears, and my whole body was shaking. Then I heard Mum scream, and I quickly slid my legs over the side of the bed and tiptoed out of my bedroom.

I was halfway down the stairs when I heard a sound behind me; as I spun round I had to reach out quickly and grab the banister to stop myself falling. It was only Asha; she was standing on the landing above me in her nightie, her eyes wide with fear. When she ran down silently to stand beside me, I put my arm around her shoulders and held her quaking body tightly against my own.

We'd just reached the bottom of the stairs when we heard a loud crash and then Mum shouted, 'That's it! I'm not taking any more. Get out. Get out of my house.' Almost immediately, Hassan came bursting out of the kitchen, his face contorted by fury, and strode down the hallway and out of the front door, without appearing even to notice that we were there.

As soon as the front door slammed behind him, Mum came out of the kitchen, too. She stopped for a moment and looked in the mirror in the hallway, raising her hand as she did so to touch the large, livid bruise that was already developing on her cheek. Then she saw us, shivering and indecisive at the bottom of the stairs, and she shouted at our reflections in the mirror, 'Go to bed.'

I did eventually go back to sleep, and I don't know how much later it was when I was woken up again, this time by someone banging on the front door. Instantly alert, I sat up in bed just as Mum screamed, 'You're not coming in. Go away or I'll phone the police.' For the next few seconds, I held my breath and listened, but there wasn't another sound. The silence made me more uneasy than the shouting had done, because I knew that Hassan was far too controlling and vindictive simply to have done what Mum told him to do and left. I was right: suddenly there was a loud sound like an explosion. Without giving myself time to think and be afraid, I jumped out of bed again and ran down the stairs.

I stood in the open doorway between the hall and the kitchen and watched in shocked disbelief as Hassan climbed in through the broken kitchen window. There was glass all over the floor and his hands were covered in blood, which he didn't even seem to notice.

Asha had followed me down the stairs again and was standing just behind me in the hall. I turned and whispered to her urgently, 'Go back upstairs. Go! Quickly! It's all right. It'll be okay.' I didn't believe that for a moment, but I knew I had to get my little sister out of the way of whatever was about to happen.

I'd often seen Hassan in rages so furious he appeared to be completely out of control, but I'd never seen him the way he was that night. As he climbed through the window, tearing his clothes and his skin on the jagged shards of glass that remained lodged in its frame, he was dragging with him a long metal pole. As soon as his feet hit the ground, he advanced across the kitchen, brandishing the pole above his head like some enraged warrior, pushing Mum up against the work surface, where she cowered, whimpering like a terrified child.

All my instincts told me to run up the stairs and lock myself and Asha in the bathroom. But because I think I'd always believed that if Hassan was ever angry enough, he'd be capable of killing someone, I knew I couldn't leave Mum to face him alone. He was already attacking her, punching the side of her head over and over again and, when he took a step away from her and raised the metal pole as if he was about to bring it crashing down on her skull, I ran towards them, across the broken glass that covered the kitchen floor.

Mum had reached out her hand behind her and curled her fingers around the handle of a knife, and I tried to grab Hassan's raised arm, shouting at him as I did so, 'Stop it! Please, stop it! You're going to kill her.' He didn't even look at me; his eyes were fixed on the knife Mum was holding like a dagger. As he knocked it out of her hand, he brought the metal pole crashing down on her head and her body seemed to fold almost gracefully as she sank, unconscious, to the floor.

When I screamed, I heard another voice shout too, and I spun round to see a man climb in through the kitchen window. Hassan had already gone – he must have slipped out through the front door immediately after striking the blow that I was certain had killed my mother. When the man jumped down into the kitchen and unlocked the back door, the room seemed instantly to be full of people.

A little while later, two paramedics lifted Mum's limp body on to a stretcher. Then, as I sat on the stairs and listened, our next-door neighbour described to the policemen who'd responded to her emergency phone call how Hassan had climbed over the fence at the back of the house and smashed the kitchen window.

I don't know if Sami actually did sleep through every-thing that happened that night; it seems unlikely in view of the fact that the noise had apparently woken half the neighbourhood. But it wasn't until after the police arrived and Mum had been carried out of the house to the ambulance that he came out of his bedroom. I turned and looked up at him where he stood above me on the stairs, and watched as he rubbed his eyes with his hand – and then went back into his room and closed the door.

Later, when the house was quiet again, a neighbour sat beside me on the stairs and gently picked all the pieces of glass out of the soles of my blood-stained feet. When she'd washed them in a bowl of warm water and disinfectant, she told me to go to bed and try to sleep. Despite the fact that I didn't think I'd even be able to shut my eyes after everything that had happened, the last thing I remember hearing before exhaustion washed over me was the sound of someone hammering plywood over the broken kitchen window.

The ambulance men had assured me before they took Mum out of the house that, despite the amount of blood that had flooded out of the wound on her head, she wouldn't die. I don't think I really believed them until she came home from hospital the next day, her face so battered and swollen that she was barely recognisable.

What happened that night was traumatic for all of us, and for weeks afterwards I had nightmares about it, as well as about how differently it *could* have ended. But I was fifteen years old and I'd been having nightmares since I was seven, so I was used to them, and I knew that not even nightmares mattered now that Hassan had gone.

Every morning after Hassan had left, I'd wake up with the same feeling of dread I'd had since he first came to live with us. Then, as I lay in bed waiting for my mind to surface into consciousness, I'd feel as if some sort of gas was seeping into my body, making it lighter until I was almost floating, because I'd remember that Hassan wasn't there any more. I would never again hear his voice calling me from upstairs, or have to stifle the silent scream that seemed to swell inside me every time I saw the handle of my bedroom door turn at night. Suddenly *everything* seemed different and, as I flung back the covers on my bed, I'd tell myself, 'I'm free; he's gone' – although even knowing that that was true didn't make it any easier to believe.

A few days after what turned out to be Hassan's last attack on any of us, Mum told me that, despite what the police had clearly wanted her to do, she'd refused to press charges against him. I was disappointed, but I wasn't really surprised by her decision. He *should* have had to answer for what he'd done to Mum – and for what he'd been doing to Sami, Asha and me for so long; the most important thing, however, was that he'd gone. I was prepared to trade his getting away with it for having him out of our lives forever.

A couple of weeks later, when I got home from school, Mum followed me into the kitchen and said, 'I'm thinking of getting back with him.' She sounded like a naughty child who knows she's done something wrong and, for a moment, I didn't understand what she meant. When I did, and as a spasm of pain twisted my stomach, I almost shouted at her, 'You're not serious? I can't believe you'd do that. If you don't care what he does to *you*, what about us? Mum, no! How can you even think about having him back?'

Mum didn't look at me as she answered, 'Well, a woman needs a man in this country.' It was something she'd said hundreds of times before when Hassan was living with us, as if it explained or even excused the terrible wrong she was doing us by allowing him to beat and bully us. But it had *never* excused *or* explained it, and I could feel anger rising up inside me, pushing ahead of it the hot tears of hurt that filled my eyes and then spilled over on to my cheeks.

For a moment, I stood looking at my mother, trying to think of *something* I could say that would make her change her mind. And then I saw the stubborn, sullen expression on her face and knew that I'd be wasting my breath. It wouldn't be the first drastically misguided decision she'd made that had had an irreversibly detrimental effect on all our lives, and I was certain it wouldn't be the last. Even so, I couldn't believe she had so little regard for us that she was actually considering inviting that monster back into our home.

I walked quickly out of the kitchen and ran up the stairs, bursting through the door into Asha's bedroom and throwing myself down in the chair beside the bed, where she was sitting with an open book balanced on her knees.

'What's wrong?' she asked, turning down the corner of the page she'd been reading and putting the book on the bed beside her.

Asha was eleven years old, and for as long as I could remember I'd been trying to protect her against all the bad things that had happened in our lives. So I don't think I'd have said anything to her at all if I hadn't been so upset by my conversation with Mum.

'I can't believe what Mum just told me,' I said, my voice muffled by my tears. 'She's thinking about letting him come back to live with us, which really means she's already decided that that's what she's going to do. I just can't bear it.'

'I know,' Asha sighed. 'She told me.'

'Doesn't she understand?' I asked. 'Doesn't she realise that he's a seriously bad man?'

'I know,' Asha said again as she handed me a tissue, 'but I suppose he's her husband now and if that's what she wants, there isn't much any of us can do about it.'

I blew my nose loudly, took a deep breath and told my sister, 'I mean that he's a *seriously* bad man. Not just because he hit us, or even because of what he did to Sami. I ...' I hesitated and swallowed a few times to try to get rid of the lump that had formed in my throat like some physical embodiment of the terrible secret I'd been keeping for so long. And then, at last, I said, 'He *did* things to me. Ever since he came to live with us, he did terrible things that I haven't ever told *anyone* about.'

Asha looked at me steadily for a moment and then she narrowed her eyes and asked, in a voice that sounded coldly suspicious, 'What do you mean? What sort of things? He did things to all of us.'

'No, not *those* things,' I told her. 'I don't mean the violence and the beatings.' My eyes drifted away from Asha's face as I unlocked the dark room in my soul where the secret had remained for so many years. 'He did disgusting things that I didn't want Mum to know about because she'd have been so upset – things that for a long time I didn't realise stepfathers don't do to their stepdaughters and that no one should ever do to a child.'

When I looked at Asha again, the expression I could see on her face made me feel sick. I don't know how I'd expected her to react. The urgent need I'd felt for someone else to understand how important it was that Hassan didn't come back to live with us had stifled every other thought in my mind. So maybe I wasn't surprised by the disgust and angry condemnation I could see in her eyes.

'I don't believe you!' Asha almost shouted the words at me. 'Why would he have done those things to *you* and not to me?'

At first, I didn't understand what she meant. 'It wasn't my fault,' I told her, hating the pleading tone I could hear in my voice. 'I was seven years old when he started doing it. I didn't know what he was doing and he hurt Sami if I refused.'

Asha wasn't listening. Her fury was written clearly on her face as she shouted at me, 'Mum's always said that *you* were the pretty one and he's always taken more notice of you than of me. It isn't fair!' And that's when I realised she was jealous. In some bizarre misinterpretation of what I was telling her, she seemed to have translated Hassan's soul-destroying abuse of me into an expression of some sort of twisted, repulsive favouritism.

I was so shocked that at first all I could do was stare at her in open-mouthed amazement. Then I snapped at her, 'For heaven's sake, Asha! The things he did to me were *horrible*. I can't even describe what they were like or how miserable they made me feel. They were even worse than the beatings. When I didn't let him do them, *he hurt Sami*! I wanted to tell someone right from the start, but he said it had to be our secret; otherwise it would be *my* fault when everyone else suffered. That's the only reason I kept quiet for so long.'

Asha made a choking sound as she swung her legs off her bed and, as I sat huddled into the chair beside it, she stood looking down at me and shouted, 'It isn't true! He didn't like you more than he liked me.' She ran out of the bedroom and I could almost hear the resentment in the thud of her feet on the stairs.

I called after her, begging her to stop, but by the time I reached the bottom of the stairs, she'd already crashed through the kitchen door and was shouting at Mum, 'You won't believe what Zara's been saying!' And within seconds she'd exposed the terrible secret I'd been keeping for so long.

For eight years, my soul had been systematically eroded by what Hassan had done to me. Often, the only thing I'd had to hold on to was the belief that by keeping his evil secret, I was saving my brother from even worse beatings and my mother from some deep unhappiness I didn't really understand. And now, in the blink of an eye, it had all been rendered pointless, wasted effort: I'd suffered for nothing.

I'd only told Asha because I was desperate for her to understand why Hassan must *not* be allowed to come back into our house. I'd thought she'd want to protect Mum too, and that I would be able to trust her to keep the secret.

It would never in a million years have entered my mind that *anyone* would feel jealous of someone who'd been sexually abused, but I suppose Asha had no means of understanding what it really meant. If it hasn't happened to you and you can't imagine the miserable, destructive, brutal reality of it, perhaps you might feel resentful that you weren't the one who was 'chosen'. Maybe Asha felt overlooked and ignored by the man who was, after all, the only father figure she'd ever really known. I understand that now, but at the time I couldn't make sense of her reaction.

For a moment, Mum just stared at Asha with a puzzled expression on her face, as if she'd begun to talk in a foreign language Mum didn't know she could speak and didn't understand herself. And then, as comprehension slowly dawned, she turned to me and asked me, 'Why didn't you tell me?'

'I didn't know what to do,' I whispered. 'To begin with ...' I paused and wiped the back of my hand across my cheeks. 'To begin with I didn't know it *was* wrong. I hated it but I didn't know it wasn't normal. He told me that it was. Then he told me that I mustn't tell anyone because ...'

I looked at my mother, silently willing her to say something that would make everything all right, something that would make it clear to me that she knew it hadn't been my fault and that she was sorry beyond words for what Hassan had done to me. Instead, she looked away from me and asked, in a voice that made it sound more like a statement than a question, 'He didn't do … *that*, did he?'

At fifteen years old, I had only very recently realised that what Hassan had been doing to me meant I wasn't a virgin. I knew that my virginity was very important to Mum, who was forever telling us, 'If you're not a virgin, you'll never find a husband.' So I hesitated for only a second or two before telling her, 'I don't want to talk about it.'

I expected her to insist but, as I braced myself for the tears I knew were coming, she shrugged her shoulders and said, 'Oh, okay. Well, that's all right then. You'll be able to get married. That's good.' Then she sighed and added ruefully, 'I suppose I can't really take him back now.'

And that was it; that was all she had to say on the matter. As far as my own mother was concerned, it was over, finished and dealt with. It was a pity she wouldn't be able to get back together with Hassan, but I expect she consoled herself with the thought that it was a sign that the time had come for her to move on. After all, he'd hit her several times during the final few weeks he'd lived with us, and there was no way she would have continued to put up with that. So perhaps, deep down, she accepted that it was for the best.

For me, it felt as if from the moment Hassan had come back into our lives, when I was seven years old, he'd systematically and methodically stripped away my spirit, my sense of self-worth, confidence and dignity, and now my mother had destroyed the last pathetic remnants of my self-esteem. I'd thought that I was protecting her with my silence, and I'd been proud because of it. But it was now clearer than it ever had been before that she had no real interest in protecting *me*.

In my mother's eyes, my only purpose as a girl was to marry and bear children – preferably sons – for my husband. And as long as I might still be able to fulfil that destiny, it didn't really matter – to Mum or to anyone else – what I'd suffered at the hands of the man she'd brought into our house after taking us away from our father, any more than it mattered how that suffering had affected me and would continue to affect me for the rest of my life.

Mum didn't let Hassan come back, and maybe he didn't really mind, because by that time, in one way or another, she'd already given him what he'd wanted. In the early days when they'd been together, she'd provided him with financial support and a roof over his head and then, when she'd married him, he'd at last got the

British passport that was so important to him. Added to all of that, he'd had the 'bonus' of being able to have sex with both her and her young daughter whenever he felt like it.

Chapter Eleven

AFTER HASSAN HAD gone, the main worry we were left with was Sami's strange behaviour. It was clear that Mum felt guilty about it. Whereas she seemed to be able to justify or completely shut her mind to most of the ways in which she'd let her children down, I think that, whatever she might have said to the contrary, she knew that there was a connection between Hassan's physical and emotional abuse of Sami and his mental illness.

I felt desperately sorry for my brother. Even as a very young child, when he was already shy and withdrawn, all he'd ever really wanted was to be liked and approved of. But first Dad and then Hassan had ridiculed and laughed at him so that he felt inadequate. He didn't know how to be different, and it must have seemed to him that he was always going to fall short of some measure of worth he didn't understand and would have had no real hope of attaining even if he had.

Eventually, Sami was diagnosed as suffering from schizophrenia and a personality disorder. The doctors said that some of the way he behaved was controllable – just bad behaviour rather than mental illness. But he certainly didn't have any control over the hallucinations he started having even before Hassan left. It seemed almost as if he was living in a parallel universe, where everything was frightening and no one could be trusted – in fact, a world pretty much like the one he'd grown up in. In the world Sami inhabited in his mind after Hassan had left, however, he wasn't afraid of what was real; it was the things that he imagined that haunted him.

One day, when we were watching television in the living room, he glanced out of the window and then almost threw himself down on the floor, where he crouched behind the sofa and whispered, 'Look! Outside in that van … No! Don't let anyone see you looking. There are people in it watching the house. They want to kill us. They're always there. That's why I can never go outside.'

'There's no one in the van, Sami,' I told him. 'It's just a builder's van. It belongs to the builder who's working on the house across the road. I've seen him getting in and out of it. It's okay. No one's trying to kill us.'

Sami remained on the floor, hugging his knees to his chest and with a look in his eyes that made me think of a wild, hunted animal. Then he smiled a cold, smug smile and said, 'You'll see. You don't know anything. Now go and get me some lunch. I want some soup.'

I hated the rude, angry way he spoke to me, but I knew that he was ill and couldn't help it – any more than he could help the fact that he was often over-whelmed and rendered completely inactive by paranoia, or the way his fearful, distorted view of everything and everyone ruled his life. So I just shrugged and said, 'Okay, I'll ask Mum to make some soup.'

But even that made him angry, and he told me impatiently, 'No. Don't ask Mum. I didn't tell you to ask Mum. Just *magic* me some soup. Go on. Do it now. I'm warning you, you'd better magic it right now or there'll be trouble.' And when I tried to explain to my brother that it wasn't possible to 'magic' soup out of thin air, he became angry and lashed out in the way Hassan had so often lashed out at him.

The slightest thing could set Sami off. After a while, he began to attack us whenever he was angry, punching and kicking whoever happened to be nearest to him when his emotions became so confused and tangled up together that he couldn't separate one from another. I kept telling myself that it wasn't his fault and I had to forgive him, but I hated the fact that I was becoming afraid of my own brother.

I'd always believed that the bond that existed between me, Sami and Asha had been made stronger by the terrible experiences we'd shared during our childhood. I suppose I'd imagined that our attachment to each other was instinctive and that it would exist whatever happened. But now it seemed that I'd been wrong and that Sami and Asha didn't feel the same way, which just reinforced the feeling that the things I'd done because I thought I was protecting the people I loved didn't really mean anything after all.

One of the effects of Sami's paranoia was that he wanted to change bedrooms with me. I didn't really understand why but I was happy to do whatever it took to keep the peace. So when he asked me the first time, I agreed, despite the fact that it meant lugging all my possessions and several pieces of furniture down the stairs to the floor below mine and then finding places for it all in my new room.

I also agreed without argument when, a couple of days later, Sami changed his mind and said he wanted to move back into his old room. My patience was wearing a bit thin, however, when he insisted on swapping again a week after that; and the next time, I finally said no.

'That's enough, Sami,' I told him. 'I'm not doing it any more. Make up your mind which bedroom you want to sleep in and then you'll have to stick to it.'

Although I'd known he'd be annoyed, I wasn't prepared for the incandescent rage he flew into or for the way he started hitting me and punching my head with his fists. He didn't even stop when Mum ripped his clothes as she tried to pull him off me and, luckily, distracted him just enough for me to be able to escape and run to the toilet where I locked the door.

I was still leaning against the toilet door, shaking, when I heard Mum scream and I knew that Sami had turned his indiscriminate fury on her. So then I *had* to come out of the toilet and try to help her. When she managed to dial 999, Sami was taken away in an ambulance to a mental hospital, where he was sectioned and remained for several weeks.

Despite feeling a sense of relief when Sami had gone, and knowing that he'd come within a hair's breadth of going too far that day and really hurting one of us, I was scared – not least about what they'd do to him at the hospital. For as long as I could remember, Sami had always been full of fears and anxieties, and I could only imagine how terrified he must be now. I was also afraid that he might never be well again, or that he might even die, and then I'd have lost him forever. And at the same time I was frightened about what would happen when he came home. I knew that if he wasn't 'cured' at the hospital, we'd have to continue to live with his abuse, because Mum would continue to take his side and wouldn't protect Asha and me against him. I was tired of being in danger all the time, and of feeling trapped and powerless to do anything about it. It seemed that everything had gone wrong: it was supposed to be better now Hassan had left, but it wasn't.

Little seemed to have changed when Sami came home again, however. It wasn't long before he stopped taking the medication he'd been prescribed, and then his paranoia continued to grow until he was afraid of everything and everyone, including his own family. 'The only way I'll ever really be safe is if you guys are all finished off,' he told us. 'Then I won't have to worry about you trying to kill me while I'm asleep.'

So *I* was afraid of *him* too, although at the same time I felt desperately sorry for him. Whereas the fears

I'd had for as long as I could remember had been real and had, for all practical purposes, evaporated on the day Hassan left, Sami's were imagined and locked inside his mind, which meant that there was no way of rationalising and explaining them so that he could at least trust the people who really did love him.

One day, without any provocation or apparent reason, he suddenly grabbed Asha around the throat and started shouting, 'She's in on it. I'm going to kill her.' Asha was struggling and choking and I was trying to calm Sami down, pleading with him to let her go and telling him, 'She's not *in on it*, Sami – whatever *it* is. I promise she doesn't want to hurt you. She loves you.' Eventually, Mum and I managed to distract him just enough for Asha to be able to loosen his frenzied grasp around her neck and escape.

We ran upstairs, our hearts racing, and when we'd locked ourselves in the bathroom, we stood with our ears pressed against the door, listening for the sound of Sami's footsteps on the stairs. But it was his voice we heard first, shouting, 'That's it. I've had enough now. I'm not taking this any more. I'm going to kill you all.' He started banging on the door with his fists, screaming for us to come out. All we could do was push against it with all our strength and pray that he didn't manage to break it down, because although he was still thin and looked as if a puff of wind could blow him over, his illness and the anger that seemed to result from it gave him a physical power he hadn't had before.

Despite the fact that he did calm down on that occasion and, eventually, on many similar occasions too, I was sure it was just a matter of time before he really hurt one of us – or maybe even killed us.

When Sami first went to hospital, after Hassan had beaten him up so badly that day, Mum had told the doctor he must have been involved in a drunken brawl and that he was 'off the rails'. It had seemed particularly unfair at the time, because Sami never went out and never got drunk. But that changed now too, and he began to get into trouble.

After he'd left school, Sami didn't get a job and he wasn't interested in going to college, which was what Mum kept trying to persuade him to do. He just sat around the house, in his room or watching television, and every so often he'd go out in the evening and not come home again until the following morning.

When Mum was sent a new credit card, she'd put it in the little case in her bedroom where she kept her personal papers and important letters, as well as the money she earned from sewing jobs, for which she was always paid in cash. A few days later, she found that the credit card, the letter containing her PIN and £300 in cash had disappeared. She knew immediately that Sami had taken them. When she challenged him about it, he shrugged and told her, 'I spent it on a lady.'

'What do you mean?' Mum asked him. 'What sort of *lady*?'

'Just a lady,' Sami answered. 'A lady who's teaching me things.'

'A prostitute!' Mum shouted at him, instantly furious. 'Is that what you're telling me? That you spent my money on a prostitute?'

Sami giggled like a naughty little boy, but when Mum continued to shout at him and to tell him how angry she was to think about her hard-earned money being spent on 'that', he eventually snarled at her, 'Get out of the way, woman. I'm watching television.'

I saw Mum glance towards the coffee table where Sami always dropped his wallet just before he sat down to watch TV, and my heart began to race as she bent down quickly and picked it up.

'What are you doing?' Sami demanded. Despite the quiet way he spoke, his voice resonated with dangerous threat.

'I'm taking my credit card,' Mum told him, hunching her shoulders and turning her back towards him as she opened the wallet and pulled out the card. 'You're not well, Sami. People realise that and they take advantage of you. It isn't safe for you to carry around large amounts of cash or a credit card.'

She was still speaking when Sami leapt to his feet and grabbed her by the hair, yanking her head to one side so sharply and with such force I thought for a moment he might have broken her neck. Then he pushed her down on to the sofa and shouted at her, 'Give it back to me – now! If you don't give me the card this minute, I'll kill you.'

Shaking with fear, Asha and I tugged at his arms and tried to pull him off her. But his fury seemed to have given him an almost superhuman strength and we couldn't break his grip on Mum. I was just beginning to think that he was going to carry out his threat and kill her and there was nothing we could do to prevent it, when he let go of her abruptly. Pushing us away, he shouted, 'You wait. I'm going to get something now and beat you *all* to death.' Then he ran out of the living room and we could hear the thud of his footsteps on the stairs.

Before he'd even reached the landing, I threw myself

against the living-room door, and Asha and Mum came to stand beside me. We listened anxiously to the sound of doors being banged open and shut above us and waited for Sami to come back. When he did, we held the door of the living room closed while he screamed at us, wild, nonsense words that were somehow more chilling than real, comprehensible threats would have been.

He began to thump on the door and batter it with something, and we could hear the wood splintering and cracking with each blow. Although Sami was small and skinny and there were three of us on our side, every time he hit it, the door opened – not very much, just an inch or two, but enough to make us realise that we wouldn't be able to hold out against him for very long.

'Sami!' I shouted, doubting whether he would be able to hear me above the thudding and the terrible, animal-like noises he was making. 'Sami, stop hitting the door. Just listen to me for a moment. I'll get the card from Mum. But you have to stop what you're doing and go upstairs. I'll get it back for you if you calm down.'

'It's too late,' he yelled. 'Even if you *do* get it back for me, I'm still going to kill you for letting her take it.'

Eventually, whatever was fuelling his anger must have been exhausted, and we heard him stomping up the stairs. Then his bedroom door slammed shut and, after waiting several minutes to make sure he'd really gone, we opened the door of the living room and dared to venture out.

'You've *got* to do something,' I told Mum later that evening. 'It isn't fair on us and it isn't fair on Sami. He's ill and he needs help.' Mum just clicked her tongue, sucked her breath in sharply through her teeth and refused to talk about it and, once again, I felt let down by her and bemused by her inexplicable refusal to act – if only so that we could feel safe in our own home.

After Hassan had gone, all I'd wanted – for all of us – was peace and quiet and to be able to sit on the sofa in the living room in the evenings and watch television knowing that the only frightening things that were going to happen would be on the screen. I wanted to be able to relax and not have to be constantly alert, watching and listening for the first signs and sounds of impending trouble.

I'd hated Hassan for the way he'd treated us and when he left I felt a huge sense of relief. It seemed, however, that without Hassan there Sami finally felt free to release the rage that must have been boiling inside him for so many years. I understood how damaged he was and I sympathised with the way he must have felt; what I *couldn't* understand was why he thought it was all right to vent his anger on *us* and to make us suffer even more than we'd already done.

I kept telling myself that Sami was ill, but I couldn't bear the prospect of having to continue to live with the constant threat – and reality – of more physical abuse. Once again, my body was covered in bruises – this time inflicted on me by my own brother – and, once again, Mum didn't do anything to protect me.

I knew there was another, better, way to live; I'd lived it myself until the age of seven and, since then, I'd seen it on television. I used to love watching programmes like *Little House on the Prairie* and *The Waltons*, in which nice families did 'normal' things together and, even when bad things happened, the parents always took care of the children, were kind to them and, clearly, really cared about them. I liked watching sad films, too, as long as they had a happy ending, because they made me believe that things *could* change – even for me.

Now, though, I felt as if I was trapped in the continuous loop of a nightmare from which I was never going to escape.

*

One evening, Sami started to rant wildly and incoherently about something – or, more likely, about nothing at all. After he'd punched me, I told Mum, 'I can't stand this any more. I'm leaving. I'm going to walk out of the door and go.' And a few minutes later, I walked out of the house into the dark and the rain.

I didn't want to leave home. What I really wanted was for Mum to say, 'No, don't go. I'll make Sami stop.' But she just stood at the front door watching me impassively as I walked down the path towards the pavement. As I opened the gate she called after me, 'Don't be stupid. You've got nowhere to go. You'd better come back inside.'

'If he does it again, I'm going to call the police,' I told her as I turned back towards the house.

'You are *not* going to call the police,' she said, angry at last – bizarrely, with me, not with Sami for what he'd done.

'Well, in that case, I'm going to go to the doctor and show him my bruises,' I retorted. 'And then *he'll* tell the police.'

Mum made me promise not to do what I'd threatened. So Sami continued to live in his own confused and confusing world, where everything either frightened him or made him furious. And I tried to come to terms with being afraid of my own brother and with having to lock myself in the bathroom at regular intervals while he pounded on the door and threatened to kill me – always for some reason that I was sure made no more sense to him than it did to me.

Asha was different. She didn't have my instinct to placate and to smooth things over. When she was attacked she fought back – and she kept trying to make Mum do something about Sami. She'd tell Mum angrily, as I had often done, 'What you're doing is wrong. You're putting Sami first because you feel guilty about what Hassan did to him and because he's ill. That's not fair. What about feeling guilty for what happened to me and to Zara and for what's still happening to us because you're allowing Sami to hurt us?' And Mum just said what she always said: 'Sami's ill.'

Eventually Asha took matters into her own hands. When Sami tried to strangle her one day, she went to school, showed the bruises to one of her teachers and never came home again.

The teacher told the headmistress, who contacted Social Services. Asha was whisked away that very day to live with a foster family, who were good to her and who she stayed with until she left school, went to college and was old enough to live in a flat on her own.

At first, I was glad Asha had told someone. When a social worker came to the house to talk to Mum and me about the allegations Asha had made about Sami, I thought it would mean he'd finally get the help he so desperately needed. But Mum refused to discuss Sami's behaviour with the social worker, and she begged me before he came not to say anything either.

'What will happen to me if you leave home, too?' she pleaded tearfully. 'I'll be left here on my own with Sami. Don't say anything, *please*.' And once again I felt guilty for having been so selfish as even to consider doing something that might make *my* life easier and possibly hers a bit harder.

Mum was sitting beside me in the living room when the social worker asked me whether what my sister had told them about Sami's behaviour affected me too.

'Well, he *is* very violent sometimes,' I said. 'And …'

Mum gave a nervous laugh and interrupted me, saying, 'Oh, it's nothing major, is it, Zara? You make it sound far worse than it really is.'

For a moment I didn't answer; I just looked down at my hands, which were clenched together tightly in my lap, and then I whispered, 'No, not really major.' With my next breath I inhaled the weight of hopeless defeat that had already settled in my stomach when I added, 'Everything's fine, really.'

'What about all the things your sister told us?' the social worker asked me. 'Are you saying that they aren't true? Or perhaps it's just that your brother doesn't treat you the way he treated her?'

'I … I don't know,' I muttered, glancing up at my mother, who looked steadily back at me with an unreadable expression on her face.

I think I expected the social worker to ask me more questions, particularly as he must have realised that it was impossible for me to speak openly with my mother sitting right beside me. He was a man, an Indian as it happened, so perhaps he didn't recognise the dynamic that existed between my mother and me, because he just shrugged his shoulders, closed the file of papers on the table in front of him and said, 'Well, okay. That's fine.' Then he opened his briefcase, dropped the papers into it, and left.

The investigation that followed Asha's complaint did result in Sami being sectioned again, and he spent six weeks in a psychiatric unit. But, again, when he came home he stopped taking his medication and, before long, Mum and I had to struggle once more to cope with the physical expression of the uneven battle he was constantly fighting with his mental demons.

I missed Asha when she left and, when I visited her at her foster home, I felt envious of her for having escaped to live a well-ordered life with a kind, cheerful, well-adjusted family, while I'd allowed what could well have been my only opportunity to do the same thing to slip through my fingers. I often wished I'd spoken out, as Asha did. But Hassan had long ago stripped away all my confidence.

Sami didn't often hit Mum, so I was the one who usually had to bear the brunt of his attacks. And although I still loved him and I knew he couldn't help it – or, at least, some of it – I sometimes told Mum, 'You've got to get him out of here. It isn't fair to make me live like this.' Then she'd take his side, as she'd always done, and I'd do what *I'd* always done and accept it.

For some reason, my ability to act in my own defence was still hampered by what I saw as my duty to try to make things better for other people – particularly for Mum. Trying to make things better for my mother, however, was – as it always had been – an uphill struggle, not least because she seemed to have an unerring instinct for doing whatever was most likely to make things worse for herself.

The one thing I didn't understand about what Asha had done when she'd shown her teacher the bruises Sami had inflicted on her, was that she'd never said anything to anyone about Hassan's beatings and the injuries *he'd* caused her. I suppose part of the reason was that she was a teenager by the time Sami became really ill and started acting violently towards us, so she had more confidence than she'd had when she was younger and Hassan had lived with us.

I asked her about it eventually, when we were both grown up. She just shrugged, as if the answer was obvious, and said, 'Hassan was the closest thing to a dad I ever remember having. I was too young when we left home to have any lasting memories of our real dad.' Perhaps the fact that that was true and that Asha didn't remember the normal life we'd had when we lived with Dad explains why she sometimes struggles with feelings of depression.

It was inevitable that Hassan's aggressive, cruel behaviour towards Sami, Asha and me when we were young was going to have long-term negative effects on us all. I think I'd hoped, however, that because Asha was the youngest and, initially at least, was mostly excluded from his physical assaults, she'd escape relatively unscathed. It was an unrealistic hope, I realise now, but it still makes me sad to know that she isn't really happy and that I wasn't able to protect my little sister.

I think I sometimes used to envy Asha because, being so much younger than Sami and I, she spent a lot of time alone with Mum when we were at school, which gave her some degree of protection against Hassan's violence. But what I hadn't previously realised was that because she didn't remember living with Dad, she had no basis for comparing our life with Hassan, so when she grew up and had to live in the real world, she understood even less about it than I did. In fact, normality was so distorted in the environment we lived in that I can remember sometimes thinking it was unfair when I did something that put Hassan in a good mood and Asha shared in the 'reward'. For example, occasionally Hassan might say to me, 'Because you did that, I'm going to take you to McDonalds,' which was a huge treat because normally we were never taken anywhere. Sometimes I'd complain to him, 'You make me do things I don't want to do, and you treat Asha like a daughter. Why am I different? I don't understand why I have to do something like that before I can go to McDonalds and then, when I do, everyone else gets the treat that I've earned.' But there was never any point complaining about anything Hassan did: he'd just shrug his shoulders and say, 'That's just the way it is. Get used to it.' And I knew from experience that if I questioned him too persistently, he'd take Asha out and buy her a present, just to spite me.

To Asha, however, those occasions – rare as they were – were simply unexpected treats. So I suppose it wasn't really surprising that her feelings towards Hassan were different from mine.

What I do find it difficult to forgive is the fact that as soon as Dad realised Mum definitely wasn't going to go back to him, he didn't bother to keep in touch with his children. And because he lost contact with us, there was no one to look out for us or protect us when we were delivered into the hands of Hassan.

Despite the shame Mum was considered to have brought on herself, her own and Dad's families when she left Dad, she'd stayed in touch with the wife of one of his brothers. One day, when I was sixteen, my aunt contacted Mum to tell her that Dad's dad was very ill and wanted to see all his family – including her – before he died. So we went to visit our aunt and uncle, and to see the cousins we hadn't seen for nine years.

I think part of the reason my aunt was keen for Mum to visit them at that time, after she and Hassan had split up, was because Dad had never given up hope that she'd go back to him. So, for the sake of a possible reconciliation, his family was prepared, if not to forgive and forget, at least to relegate to the past the shame Mum had brought on them. For me, however, going to our aunt and uncle's house was like stepping into some surreal film set.

Before Dad had lost first one house to Mum and then the other because he couldn't pay the mortgage after she'd left him, his brothers had gone through both houses like a plague of locusts and taken everything – furniture, clothes, toys, rugs; anything they could either sell or use themselves. So when we visited our cousins, we saw, in pride of place in their living room, the massive fish tank I remembered clearly having been in our house when I was young. I recognised some of the rugs too, and there was a photograph on a table of one of my cousins when she was little, wearing a pink and purple coat, which I could distinctly remember used to be *my* favourite coat.

No one else seemed to think there was anything odd about our cousins showing us how well all the things we'd had to leave behind fitted in to their home. But it felt to me as though I was being shown a glimpse of the life *I* should have lived – the life I *would* have lived if Mum hadn't run away to be with Hassan.

Chapter Twelve

MUM AND HASSAN split up just a few months before I was due to take my GCSEs. I'd already been predicted poor grades – mostly Ds and Es, with the best one being a C. In some ways, it wasn't really surprising, because even after we came back to London, we didn't stay in any house for more than about eighteen months, so I hadn't been at my secondary school for very long by the time Hassan left. But suddenly, with him gone, it felt like a new beginning and I decided to try to turn things around.

Over the previous few years – since we'd first gone to Manchester – I'd lost the ability to concentrate in class, as well as the confidence to believe that I could do well. Fortunately though, I had just enough memory of the school I'd gone to in London until I was seven, where my teachers always praised and encouraged me, to know that I wasn't really stupid.

Although I didn't really think there was enough time left before my exams to make much of a difference, I knew I could do better than I had been doing. So, for those last few weeks, I knuckled down and worked as hard as I could and, to everyone's amazement – not least my own – I passed all eight subjects with A and B grades.

When the GCSE results arrived, I was *really* proud of myself. I felt that I'd finally achieved something, and I began to wonder if perhaps I could have a good life after all. After I'd taken the exams, I left school and went to college to do A-levels, and then I applied for university.

It seemed that the next few years were mapped out for me, but when I worked as a sales assistant in a shop during the summer holiday after I'd left college, I enjoyed the work itself and the feeling of independence it gave me so much that I decided not to go to university after all and I applied for another job, this time in an office.

While I was at college doing my A-levels, my life had settled into a new normality, which was relatively unremarkable except when it was punctuated occasionally by Sami's aggressive outbursts. And then Mum met another man – an Indian who'd recently arrived in England as an illegal immigrant and who had a wife and three children at home in India.

Mum may not have loved my dad – that's the risk of arranged marriages – but he didn't treat her badly, and most of the horrible things that have happened in her life have been the direct result of her own choices. The kindest thing I can say about my mother is that she has never really grown up: in many respects, she's still the naïve thirteen-year-old girl who came to England to marry her cousin. If I'm *not* trying to be kind, however, I'd say that she's selfish and foolishly impulsive. After Hassan had left and Mum had found out that he'd been sexually abusing me, she'd realised she couldn't have him back, even though she wanted to. So she'd filed for divorce. She didn't mention the abuse to anyone, because it was an embarrassment to her, and Hassan accepted her request for a divorce without question – after all, he had his British passport so he didn't need Mum any longer. And it turned out he was already making arrangements to bring a young bride over from Morocco.

You'd have thought that after everything that had happened as a result of her relationship with Hassan, Mum would be almost obsessively cautious about whom she got tied up with next, but she was resolutely determined to do whatever she wanted to do and to hell with the consequences.

Mum didn't go out to work, didn't have any friends and didn't socialise, other than talking occasionally to neighbours and sometimes having tea with the Asian couple who lived across the road. When the couple visited her one day, they said they wanted her to meet their friend, a man who, before coming to the UK, had been born and lived in the same place in India that Mum came from.

'It seems like I've known him all my life,' Mum simpered after she'd met him for the first time. 'He doesn't seem like a stranger at all.'

It was on Rahul's second visit that he offered to give her £10,000 if she'd marry him. 'I want to bring my family to this country,' he said, 'and to do that I must have a British passport.' Fortunately, Mum had just enough good sense to refuse, and to tell him, 'I've already been divorced twice. I can't marry again. It would bring too much shame on me and on my family.'

But Rahul kept asking her and, within hours of refusing him, the little good sense she seemed to have had flew out of the window and she told him, 'Marrying for money would be shameful, whereas marrying for love would be a completely different thing.' So Rahul confided in her that he didn't really love his wife at all and that the *real* reason he'd asked

Mum to marry him wasn't because he wanted a passport and the opportunity to give his family a new and better life in England; it was because he'd fallen in love with her as soon as he'd met her.

When Mum told me what he'd said and that she thought she might marry him after all, I was completely astounded. 'You can't be serious!' I said. 'You can't marry him! You've only known him for a week. You don't know anything about him. It's ridiculous. If you like him, just go out with him.'

'I can't *go out* with him!' she exclaimed, as if *I'd* been the one to say something shocking. 'Going out with him would be a shameful thing to do.'

I might have laughed if I hadn't felt so exasperated and depressed by what she was saying. Instead, I sighed as I told her, 'You've broken so many rules already that I don't think there's anything you could do now that would make anyone bat an eyelid. You're already an outcast, so you might as well go out with him and not worry about what people will think.' What I wanted to *shout* at her was, 'After everything that's happened, why on earth would you even consider bringing a stranger into our home?' But I didn't; I kept my hurt to myself. Mum knew I'd been sexually abused by Hassan for eight years, and she knew too – however much she chose to deny it – that Hassan was at least partly responsible for Sami's illness. Despite what she knew, however, it didn't seem to cross her mind to wonder how either of us might feel about the prospect of another man living in our home.

After my grandfather had died, I'd kept in touch with his wife – my step-grandmother – and I went to stay with her for a weekend. The arrangement had been made before Mum had met Rahul and when the time came I was glad to be escaping for a couple of days. I would have been considerably less happy, however, if I'd known what was going to take place in my absence.

When I got home from my weekend away, Rahul had moved in and Mum announced with a girlish giggle that they were married.

'He was only sending money to his wife in India because he cares about his children. So he divorced her and married me,' Mum told me. Despite sounding almost smugly confident, she didn't look at me as she said it.

I knew there was no point saying aloud the words that were in my head. Mum always believed what she wanted to believe and only ever saw what she wanted to see. Clearly, she had either not understood or had chosen to ignore the fact that it isn't possible to get a divorce within just a few days. So all I said was, 'You could get locked up for what you've done.' As I wiped away the tears of hurt and disappointed frustration that were stinging my eyes, Mum turned away from me and picked up an envelope full of photographs of her most recent wedding.

I didn't really say anything more about it until a few days later when we had a massive row and I told her, 'I'm still living in the house and after everything that's happened, you've brought some stranger to live here with us – a man you've known for less than a month. Surely you can see that that's bizarre and irresponsible by any standard?' But, of course, she couldn't.

Suddenly, I could see that all the violence, beatings and abuse Sami, Asha and I had suffered for all those years had been, purely and simply, the result of what *she'd* done. I didn't blame her for leaving Dad to be with Hassan; I assumed it was something she'd felt she had to do for reasons I couldn't – and probably wouldn't ever – understand. I *did* blame her, however, for *staying* with Hassan – and, more importantly, for making us stay with him when he treated us so badly. I'd told myself countless times that she must have felt she *had* to stay after she'd left Dad and become an outcast to both their families. But in view of what she'd just done and the fact that she'd wilfully put us in the path of potential hurt and danger again, I wasn't so sure that that was the real reason she hadn't left Hassan after all.

And then, having married Rahul without knowing anything about him and having brought him into the house to live with us, she went away on holiday, taking Sami with her and leaving me alone with her new husband.

After the summer when I'd left college and had worked for a while in a shop, I'd got the job I'd applied for as office junior in the legal department of a large company. Because I was out at work every day, I had very little contact with Rahul while Mum was away, until one night, when he got drunk.

I'd spent most of the evening in my bedroom, reading and listening to music, and when I went downstairs to get a glass of milk, he was in the kitchen. In the few days I'd known him, we'd developed a polite yet distant relationship and despite objecting to the *fact* of him living with us, I didn't have any real objection to him personally – other than believing that he'd lied to Mum in order to persuade her to marry him.

As I walked into the kitchen, I smiled vaguely without looking directly at him – and the next thing I knew, he'd thrown his arms around my neck and was hugging me.

'I really miss your mum,' he told me, his voice thick with the tears of self-pity that come so easily to self-centred people when they're drunk.

'Well, she'll be back soon,' I said briskly, twisting my shoulders and trying to break away from his embrace.

'Ah, I miss her *so* much,' he sighed and, as he spoke, he slid his hands down my back.

Immediately, my whole body became tense and my head seemed to be full of the loud, booming sound of my own pulse as I shouted at him, 'What are you doing? Get off me!' I was crying as I ran up the stairs to my bedroom and stood with my back pressed against the door.

I didn't see Rahul the next morning before I went out to work and I didn't ever confront him about what he'd done that night. We simply avoided each other until Mum came home and then, a few days later, I moved out.

I'd just received my first full pay packet from my new job when I looked in the local newspaper for a room to let, went to see one, paid the deposit, went home to pack my stuff and left.

As I walked out of the front door, clutching a couple of black bin-liners containing almost all my worldly possessions, Mum was clearly upset. She didn't try to stop me leaving, however, and as soon as I was sitting in the taxi that was waiting for me outside the house, I burst into tears and cried all the way to my new home. I was escaping and it should have felt like a new start; but old habits die hard and I still loved my mum and wanted her to be happy more than I wanted almost anything else. This time though, despite the fact that I felt devastated and guilty because *I* was the cause of her distress, I knew I had to stand my ground and, for once, put myself first.

I didn't tell Mum where I was going until a few days later, when I phoned and gave her the address. Even then she remained convinced that she was entirely in the right. To Mum, moving a man into the house who she'd married within days of meeting him was a 'normal' thing to do and she simply couldn't see my point of view at all. She thought I was being totally unreasonable about Rahul: I'm sure she didn't even try to imagine how the presence in our home of a man I didn't know might make me feel after everything that had gone before.

The truth was that with a man in the house, Mum was happy again, so she didn't need her children. It seemed that it took the presence of a man to make her visible, even to herself, and she did everything for

Rahul, including getting up early every morning to make sure he had a freshly ironed shirt to wear.

The room I'd rented was small and, apart from the bed, the only furniture in it was an old, rotten chair that was so full of woodworm holes I was afraid to sit on it in case it disintegrated underneath me, and a table that had been badly painted in horrible, dirty-green-coloured paint that was already starting to peel off in little flakes. Looking back on it now, it was a horrible, depressing little room, but I thought it was wonderful. I was happy: I had a job I enjoyed; I'd made friends I really liked and who seemed to like me; I was free; and, most importantly of all, I'd achieved all those things entirely on my own.

Not long after I'd started working as an office junior, I'd begun to feel that something really important had happened to me. I finally had some control over my own life and, evenly more significantly, working with lots of 'normal' adults was giving me an insight into the lives of other people. So it wasn't long before I realised that the world was much larger than – and very different from – the place I'd always imagined in my head. It seemed that there were opportunities I hadn't even known existed and, for the first time for as long as I could remember, I believed that *my* life could be stable and uncomplicated.

I hadn't had any contact with Dad for years by that time. He talked to Sami on the phone occasionally, so I knew that he'd recently got married, having accepted at last that Mum was never going to go back to him. One day, when I was feeling miserable for some reason and wanted to talk to someone who might care about me, I phoned him.

When his new wife answered the phone, I nearly hung up. But then I realised that she sounded friendly and nice, so I told her who I was and asked if I could speak to my dad. I could hear Dad's voice in the background, indistinct at first and then more clearly as he said, 'What does she think? That I couldn't have got in touch with her myself if I'd wanted to speak to her? Tell her I'm busy. Stupid girl!'

I put the phone down quickly and tried to tell myself that it didn't matter what he thought. What value did his opinion have anyway – a man who had never cared about his own children enough to bother to stay in contact with them, even by simply sending them cards every year on their birthdays? But I still cried for a long time that night.

It was probably because of Mum's experiences with men as well as Hassan's abuse of me that I didn't have a boyfriend until I was eighteen – which was ironic after all the concerns Hassan had expressed before and after we went to Morocco about my alleged developing interest in boys.

When I met Adan, while when I was working in London, it seemed that, like Hassan, wherever Rahul's *own* moral compass might point, he felt that it was his 'duty' in his role as my stepfather to pontificate on *my* morality.

'She's got a boyfriend?' he asked Mum. 'In our culture, young women don't have *boyfriends*.' And to ensure that there could be no misunderstanding about the degree of his disgust, he spat as he said the word.

Later, choosing to forget that she'd recently got married, for the third time, to a man she'd known for just a few days, Mum told me, 'He's right. You shouldn't have a boyfriend. *I* will find you a husband and, until I do, you should not go out with boys.'

When I left home, I started to regain a very small amount of the confidence I'd once had as a young child and, in the process, I had become determined not to remain trapped in the web of my mother's selfishness. So I just laughed and told her that Adan was a nice boy and I intended to go on seeing him. What I didn't add – although I could have – was that in view of the husbands she'd chosen for *herself*, she would probably be the last person on earth who I'd allow to choose one for me.

Adan was Bengali and it was true that he was a very nice person. In fact, perhaps the most important thing about him from my point of view was that I couldn't imagine him being cruel or unkind to anyone. I wasn't attracted to him and our relationship wasn't 'serious', but I went out with him for several months because I felt comfortable and safe with him.

I know that some women who've been abused as children are drawn, like determinedly self-destructive moths to a flame, to men who treat them badly. I suppose it's all to do with growing up without any sense of self-worth, because someone's told you for years that you're worthless. Perhaps there's also an element of the subconscious 'recognition' of characteristics in the men you go out with that are familiar to you, even if those characteristics are violence and aggressive cruelty. Being treated badly is what you got used to when you were a child, so it's what you expect as an adult.

I did the opposite, however, and only went out with men who were really nice. After Adan, I met Steven, who was one of the nicest men you could ever hope to meet. I was nineteen and for the first time in my life I knew what it was like to be loved and be in love.

Gradually, with Steven's help, I began to rebuild my confidence and to lay the groundwork for the good life I was going to create for myself. I moved away from the area of London where my mother lived, got another job, which I loved, and worked hard at making some really good friends, who I'm still close to now, eleven years later. You don't ever 'forget' or 'get over' being sexually abused – or being abused in any way – and I did tell Steven that it had happened. I told him, too, that I wanted to leave it in the past because I refused to let it ruin my life. It *has* made me less trusting of people than perhaps I might otherwise have been, but the men I've had serious relationships with – all two of them! – have helped me to realise that some men *can* be trusted and relied on.

However, it began to become apparent that my mother had an uncanny knack for getting involved with men who were going to let her down and cause her pain, and one day, two years after they'd been married, Rahul packed his bag, opened the front door and walked out of the house without saying anything to anyone.

Mum was in the kitchen when she heard the door close and she ran out into the street behind him, calling his name and asking, 'Where are you going? Why are you carrying a suitcase?' Rahul barely turned his head as he told her, 'My letter from the Home Office arrived in the post this morning. I can get a passport now. Thanks for everything.' And all Mum could do was watch him walk away.

When she told the neighbours who'd introduced Rahul to her and who she'd really believed were her friends, they shrugged and said, 'There was always a chance that that was his real intention. We thought you understood.' But it seems that Mum hadn't understood at all and she was deeply hurt.

'I *really* thought it was love,' she told me afterwards, and when I realised she was heartbroken, I couldn't help feeling sorry for her, or marvelling at her capacity for self-delusion.

Wanting to put the whole experience behind her, she agreed when Rahul asked for a divorce, but it must have been hard for her when, a year later, as soon as the divorce was finalised, he brought his wife and children to England – as he'd clearly always intended to do.

I think I found Steven at a crucial period in my life and, for three years, I had a really good time with him. Everyone in his family was lovely and very kind to me. They were close to each other and clearly enjoyed spending time together – which meant that they were about as different from my very dysfunctional family as it was possible to be – and I learned a lot from them, particularly about people and about what life is really like. And then I ruined it all.

I didn't have enough self-confidence to believe that I deserved to be as happy as I was. You can't build up a sense of self-worth from absolutely zero to a good functioning level in a short space of time; the process starts almost from the moment you're born and it takes years. So I destroyed my own happiness.

Despite understanding, intellectually, that what Hassan had done to me wasn't *my* fault, I was insecure. I'd sometimes have an overwhelmingly horrible feeling that the people who cared about me thought I was nicer than I really was, and that one day they'd find out they'd been wrong, and then … I didn't know what would happen then; I just knew that thinking about it made me feel sick and frightened.

But whereas that might have been the explanation for what I did to Steven – or part of it at least – it wasn't an excuse.

Surprisingly, perhaps, the disgusting, perverted things Hassan had done to me hadn't put me off sex: I could separate having sex with someone I cared about from the sexual *abuse* that Hassan had subjected me to, which was quite different and distinct. What I think I was still confused about, however, was the relationship between sex and attention, which might be part of the reason why, one day, I kissed another man.

When Steven found out about what I'd done, he was as deeply hurt and upset as I should have known he'd be, but then he forgave me. And he did *try* to forgive me again when I subsequently slept with someone else.

I should have known better than anyone that relationships are all about trust, and that what I'd done would destroy the trust that had always existed between Steven and me. It's ironic when you think that *I* was the one who'd always been afraid to trust other people, and yet when I found someone I could rely on implicitly, I took his love and stamped all over it.

I think many people who've suffered childhood abuse have a self-destruct button. It's like a panic button, except that they don't push it to get themselves out of bad situations; they push it when the situation they're in is good, because they don't believe they deserve the good things they've been given. I knew – too late – that that was what I'd done, and when Steven and I split up, I vowed never again to treat anyone the way I'd treated him.

After that, I went out, briefly, with a couple of different guys, just casually on dates, which wasn't what I wanted, not least because I find the emotional side of relationships really difficult. I'm very stubborn, as well as sensitive and quite easily upset, and if someone hurts my feelings, I hold on to it and find it very hard to brush it off. So I'm not the easiest person to be involved with, even though I *do* try hard to rationalise the way I feel.

I was twenty-three when I met Alastair. I knew what I wanted by that time – someone decent who had the same goals and aspirations in life as I had – and it wasn't long before I began to think that Alastair might just be that person.

I'd told Steven about my childhood at quite an early stage in our relationship, but I didn't tell Alastair until we'd been going out for some time. Maybe it was because I felt that, after the way I'd hurt Steven, I wasn't as far removed and as safe from my past as I'd thought I was, so I was cautious about letting anyone else get close to me. And I was lucky, because Alastair was another good man – a man I could trust – and when I did tell him, he was gentle and understanding.

We were married in a huge house in the country. Sami was still ill, despite the medication he was taking to try to control his schizophrenia, and he wasn't well enough to come to our wedding. Asha and Mum did come, though – after Mum had made a very predictable fuss about almost everything, including not wanting to travel 'all that way' and complaining that we could have had the reception in a local Harvester restaurant. Her moans and criticisms were really all to do with the fact that she wasn't the centre of attention for once, and I came very close to telling her that I'd quite happily get married without her there, if that's what she'd prefer me to do. Of course, she enjoyed the wedding, despite herself. She'd never seen an English stately home before and she was completely amazed by the house and its beautiful gardens – so amazed, in fact, that she even went as far as admitting that it *was* a better place than a Harvester to hold a wedding reception!

I'm very happy with Alastair. I still find it difficult to trust people and I still have to struggle with the beliefs that I'm not attractive and that new people I meet aren't going to like me. Despite knowing *why* I feel that way, it's sometimes hard to overcome the habits of a lifetime and to remember that many of the 'facts' learned as a child aren't true at all.

Alastair and I rarely have rows, and being so close to someone has forced me to examine some of my own feelings and reactions. For example, not long before we were married, we were having an argument – about something fairly trivial – and I was being stubborn and insisting on getting my own way, when Alastair suddenly made a frustrated growling noise. For a moment I thought I was going to faint and, as I stood there with my heart thumping, waiting for him to lose his temper and smash something, a voice in my head kept saying, 'It's coming. Something really bad is going to happen now.'

I didn't tell Alastair how I felt. Instead, I held on to the resentment and the hurt for some time and wouldn't speak to him, until eventually he asked me, 'Surely you're not *still* in a huff?' Sometimes, even when I know I'm wrong, I find it hard to back down, and I turned away from him as I answered, 'Yep.' Instead of being cross with me, however, as I expected him to be, he laughed and said, 'I know you're sorry, really. You're just finding it difficult to say so. It's all right: I forgive you.'

I knew then that it was only because I felt so secure with Alastair that I'd had the confidence to be huffy in the first place. I'd never have done that with even my closest friend, because, with anyone else, I'm afraid of getting involved in any sort of conflict, so I always apologise and back down.

I could see that Alastair was shocked when I told him how I'd felt when we were arguing, and how, despite knowing in the rational part of my mind that he wouldn't hurt me, I'd been waiting for him to fly into a rage and maybe even hit me.

'You know I'd never do anything like that,' he told me gently.

'No, that's just it,' I said. 'I *don't* know. Just because you haven't done it yet doesn't mean …'

'I'm *so* sorry,' Alastair said, putting his arms around me and holding my head against his chest so that I could hear his heart beating. 'I didn't realise.'

A day rarely passes when I don't remember something about my childhood. I'm determined not to dwell on it or let it get me down, so I don't sit and mope about it. It's just that when something sparks a memory, I can't stop the memories flooding back into my mind, and then I have to tell myself that it's just part of my history, it's over and I have to pull myself together.

I read somewhere that people's minds try to compart-mentalise traumatic events that have happened to them, and that's what I try to do, quite consciously. Alastair can remember lots of things about his past. For example, if he hears a song, he can often recall the exact date on which he first heard it, and when I ask him how, he says, 'Because it was the day of my ex-girlfriend's sister's birthday and we went to a party at …' He can remember things that happened when he was just three or four years old too – even small, inconsequential things he did with his mother – which seems amazing to me, because when I try to think back to things that happened before I was six, my mind is almost a complete blank. The things that happened *after* I was six have blotted it all out, which means that the random images of most of the rest of my childhood – except for being at school – have nothing to anchor them in time.

Not very long ago, I had a few sessions of counselling over a period of about three months. Perhaps I should have kept going for longer, because it didn't seem to do a lot of good, but I'm not sure that there's a great deal a counsellor could tell me that I don't already know. It's really just a case of putting what I know into practice.

I probably sound to other people as though I've come through it all relatively unscathed – untouched by the evil I lived with as a child – and I know that I appear to be stable and level-headed. But the truth is that I suffer from low self-esteem and my apparent confidence is mostly an act. I hide behind what's often a bit too much make-up and it makes me uncomfortable when someone compliments me on the way I look. Because in reality I crave approval and I'm always afraid that people won't like me. I just hide it well and I've learned not to let people see when I'm sad – although that's difficult sometimes, particularly after I've had a nightmare about being abused and beaten, when I can feel low for the whole of the next day.

I still love my brother Sami. He lives down the road from Mum now, and he's often difficult and aggressive. But I know what his life has been like, so I can't really blame him, even for the things he does that are 'bad behaviour' rather than due to his illness.

Asha and I keep in contact too, even though our relationship is often tense and, I'm sure, mutually irritating.

I've never really confronted Mum about what happened with Hassan. I've sometimes tried to broach the subject with her, but she still seems to be very naïve and oblivious to what her priorities as a parent should have been. The truth is that, for whatever reason, she *did* let us down, although I don't blame her for it now – at least, not openly.

When we were little, Mum often used to talk about the things she 'had to do', and I accepted them as being imperatives in her life. Later, I used to think that if, despite speaking almost no English, she was able to find the courage to leave her husband and everyone else she knew, travel half the length of the country with three young children and start her life again, she should have been able to do whatever was necessary to protect us when she realised that her boyfriend was a violent bully. So perhaps it was because of her childlike self-absorption and poor judgement rather than her courage that we ended up in Manchester with Hassan.

It's true that Mum took us away from our father to live with a vicious, violent child abuser. But whenever I think about that, I remind myself that you can't know how someone else feels and why they make the decisions they make. I just have to try to accept that she must have had her own reasons for doing what she did, and that she didn't know what Hassan was doing to me for all those years.

Not very long ago, Mum told me that her initial dislike of Hassan when he was my parents' lodger in London had been due to the fact that he used to try to touch her when there was no one else in the house, and that one day he'd raped her. If what she said is true, it's even more difficult to understand why she allowed herself to be wooed and cajoled by him into what became a willing relationship. I suppose that, once again, the explanation lies in the fact that she had only a child's understanding of the world and the people in it, which meant that someone like Hassan could have convinced her of almost anything.

She also told me that he'd said to her one day, 'Run away with me. Why do you stay with that useless lump of a man? You are young and beautiful and you could do a lot better than *him*.'

'Ah, but who would take care of my children?' Mum had asked him with a sigh. 'What man would take on another man's children, even for the sake of a beautiful woman?'

'Why, I would,' Hassan had replied, putting his arm around her slender waist and pulling her body close to his. 'Run away with me and I'll treat your children as if they are my own. They will sit on top of my eyelashes and want for nothing.'

And she believed him.

I *have* sometimes tried to talk to her about what Hassan did to me and about the impact his beatings and sexual abuse had on me, but she acts as if she had no idea what was going on – which certainly isn't true with regard to the physical abuse – and she won't accept any responsibility for it. In fact, she turns the whole thing on its head and blames me for not telling her at the time, and if I persist in confronting her, she gets upset and then I feel mean and guilty.

In Mum's mind, apparently, she was as much a victim as we were, and trying to talk to her about it just ends up with me feeling more upset and frustrated. She doesn't want to understand and she won't accept any blame for what happened. I think it would really help me to have her acknowledgement of what I went through, but she is still so unaware of her responsibilities, so much of a child herself, that I can't see it happening.

Mum is still very naive in other ways too. She persists in getting tangled up with men who apparently find her alluring and irresistibly attractive. Amazingly, she's always tempted by the lure of love and believes them when they tell her that the fact that they want British passports has nothing whatsoever to do with their eagerness to marry her. Luckily, so far she's listened to Asha and me when we've told her that three marriages are enough for anyone, but with Mum you never know what she'll do.

Perhaps she did have reasons for leaving Dad and then staying with Hassan that made sense to her at the time. If that's the case, maybe she will explain them to me one day. Whether she does or not is her choice.

When my mother was ill recently, I realised that, whatever happened in the past, I am her daughter and she needs the support of her children, so I won't be asking her any more questions now. I can't begin to imagine her not being around. I want to make her happy – just like I did when I was a little girl – and I still live in hope that one day she'll show me in some way that she really does love me.

I don't have any contact with my dad now. Apparently, he told Sami on the phone after my wedding that I'd brought shame on the family by marrying a white non-Muslim. At first I was deeply hurt that my own father could say something so cruel and narrow-minded. But then I thought about the nature of shame and I realised that I've experienced enough misery, abuse and brutality in my life to know that it isn't inter-cultural or inter-faith marriage that's shameful. What disgraces us as human beings is the terrible, secret evil that some people inflict on those who are weaker than they are for any reason – and it's that evil that they'll be held accountable for one day by the gods of their own religion.

I have a child of my own now, who I love more than I'd ever have thought it was possible to love anyone. I was anxious when I was pregnant, because I didn't know *how* to be a mother. But, with Alastair's help and the support of his family, I'm muddling through. I live in constant terror of someone abusing my child. If anyone ever tried to, I'd make sure that they lived to regret it. In fact, I can't bear to hear about any child who's suffered abuse. If there's a story on the news, I have to turn it off, because I know that if any of the words imprint themselves on my brain, they'll be there forever. I wish I *didn't* know what children who've been abused feel and think, but I do, and I know, too, that of all the evil things people do to each other, there are few – if any – that are worse than the abuse of a child.

If you liked *Secret Evil*, you might
also want to read ...

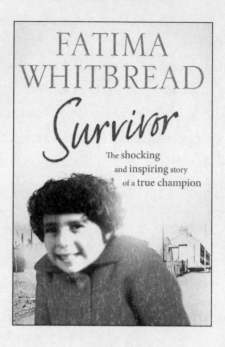

Abandonment was Fatima Whitbread's welcome to the world. It didn't get any friendlier. Fighting back from the worst possible start in life, against hopelessless, helplessness and brutality, this is the inspirational story of a woman who triumphed against all the odds.

This moving autobiography from the *I'm A Celebrity* star is available in all good bookshops from 5 July 2012, priced £7.99.

To find out more about our latest publications,
please sign up to our newsletter at:
http://www.eburypublishing.co.uk/